AF505378

Dance, Music, Theater: 250 Anecdotes and Stories

David Bruce

Published by David Bruce, 2025.

Table of Contents

Dance, Music, Theater:
250 Anecdotes and Stories

***

Copyright 2025 by Bruce D. Bruce

***

Cover Photo: Public Domain
David Garrick

***

"We devoured books as if they were popcorn. There was hardly a panhandler or fire chaser among us who didn't know Proust, Gide, Pushkin, Tolstoy, Nietzsche, and all the rest of the great scribblers in good standing."—Ben Hecht on newspapermen of the early 20th century.[1]

***

Educate Yourself
Read Like A Wolf Eats
Be Excellent to Each Other
Books Then, Books Now, Books Forever

Dedicated to My Sister Carla

Bai Juyi went to Zen master Daolin of the Tang Dynasty and asked what one must do in order to live in accord with the Tao. Daolin answered, "One must avoid doing evil, and one must do as much good as possible." Bai Juyi was surprised at the simplicity of this answer and said, "Even a child knows that." "True," replied Daolin, "even a child of three knows this but even a man of 80 fails to live up to it."

A seeker after truth once asked a wise person how to seek God. The wise person replied, "The ways to God are as many as there are created beings. But the shortest and easiest is to serve others, not to bother others, and to make others happy."

The Zen master Gisan was taking a bath. The water was too hot, so he asked a student to add some cold water to the bath. The student brought a bucket of cold water, added some cold water to the bath, and then threw the rest of the water on a rocky path. Gisan scolded the student: "Everything can be used. Why did you waste the rest of the water by pouring it on the path? There are some plants nearby which could have used the water. What right do you have to waste even a drop of water?" The student became enlightened and changed his name to Tekisui, which means "Drop of Water."

While walking along a river, two monks noticed a lettuce leaf floating downstream. "How sad," said one of the monks, who knew that Zen master Gisan lived one mile upstream. "Gizan has started to waste food." Just then, Gisan burst out of the bushes, panting and sweating, jumped into the river, and began to swim downstream after the lettuce leaf. The two monks bowed low in the direction of Zen master Gisan, and then they continued their walk.

Human beings have free will. According to the Babylonian Niddah 16b, whenever a baby is to be conceived, the Lailah (angel in charge of contraception) takes the drop of semen that will result in the conception and asks God, "Sovereign of the Universe, what is going to be the fate of this drop? Will it develop into a robust or into a weak person? An intelligent or a stupid person? A wealthy or a poor person?" The Lailah asks all these questions, but it does not ask, "Will it develop into a righteous or a wicked person?" The answer to that question lies in the decisions to be freely made by the human being that is the result of the conception.

Chapter 1: From Actors to Bathrooms

Actors

• When Gordon Davidson agreed to produce Oliver Hailey's play *Who's Happy Now?*, he asked Mr. Hailey which actress he thought would be right to play the role of the mother. Mr. Hailey said that he had written the role for an actress whom he had never met but had seen in movies: Betty Garrett. He added that Mr. Davidson might find it difficult to contact her. Mr. Davidson simply smiled, dialed a telephone number, and said, "Hello, Betty — it's Gordon. I have a playwright who says he wrote a part especially for you. Would you be willing to read it?" She did read it, and she also requested that the play be given a full production rather than be performed for only a single night — something that made Mr. Hailey happy. Mr. Hailey was also happy when he heard Ms. Garrett read the role. He thought, "That's Betty Garrett. Reading lines I wrote — and she's going to memorize them, too!" During rehearsals, Mr. Davison made a suggestion to Mr. Hailey, "You wrote that part for Betty. She's playing wonderfully — but don't you think you owe her a little more, especially in the third act?" Mr. Hailey immediately wrote a new speech for Ms. Garrett. He said, "I immediately left the room, yellow pad and pencil in hand, walked for about an hour, writing as I walked, [and] returned with what I still feel is the best speech I've ever written. Betty, of course, played it beautifully, Gordon beamed (that damn dimple [of his] grew even larger) and I learned what real collaboration meant."[2]

• Not everyone should have—or adopt—children. The first husband of actress Eileen Atkins could not have children, and since people advised them to adopt, they started to go through the process of adoption. One day, the doorbell rang, and when Ms. Atkins opened the door, an infant was on the doorstep. She immediately thought, "My God—they've delivered it." She also says, "The blood ran out of every vein. I thought this is your life, for the next 20 years, and I just did not want it." Needless to say, they did not adopt. (The infant actually belonged to a woman who was going door to door selling cloths. Ms. Atkins did not notice her at first glance.) By the way, another thing that Ms. Atkins does not care for is someone stroking her head when she is ill. She told fellow actress Judi Dench, "I can see it, I'll be lying there, paralyzed, and my husband will be stroking my brow, and I shan't be able to protest at the last." A problem-solver, Ms. Dench gave her a silver disk on a chain. The silver disk had written on it, "Don't stroke my head." And for Ms. Atkins' birthday, Ms. Dench sent her a cake with "Don't stroke my head" written in icing on it. Ms. Atkins thanked her with a limerick: "There once was a Dame name of Jude / who thrilled the entire multitude / she was fond of a joke and often a poke / but thought frottage was really quite rude." Ms. Atkins says about the limerick, "It's not terribly witty, but it's got the word 'frottage' in it, which I learnt last week and am extremely proud of. For frottage's sake, I share it."[3]

• Here are some David Garrick stories: 1) David Garrick, the famous 18th-century actor, was short, standing only five-feet-four-inches tall. Mr. Garrick and Spranger Barry once engaged in a theatrical competition. They both played Romeo at two theaters located near each other and tried to attract larger audiences than the other. Garrick's lack of height caused a wit to compose this epigram: "So reversed are the notions of Capulet's daughters, / One loves a whole length, the other three-quarters." 2) When Samuel Foote was making some puppets, he was asked if they would be life-sized. Mr. Foote mischievously replied, "Oh, no, not much larger than Garrick." 3) Mr. Garrick once entered a coach, but the coach driver refused to move until three other passengers had climbed aboard. Therefore, Mr. Garrick surreptitiously got out of the coach three times and ostentatiously—appearing to be three different people—got aboard it. Thinking the coach was full, the driver drove off. 4) Like many great actors, the great 18th-century actor David Garrick had a rubbery face with which he could create many different expressions. Once, as Sir Joshua Reynolds was trying to paint him, Mr. Garrick changed his expression each time the famous artist looked at him.[4]

• Many people think that acting is a glamorous profession, but often it is not. Eva Green acted in a play for a while, but she hated it. She explains, "I was in this play, and I didn't get on with the director and didn't like the play. It was very grotesque, you know? Too much make-up and wigs and I was playing, like, this coquette. I was on stage for most of the time apart from three minutes when I was allowed to go off and pee in a bucket. And for those three minutes I was sitting on a bucket, peeing and crying at the same time. Oh, it was terrible. It was a nightmare. I hated it so much." By the way, her father, although his main job is being a dentist, acted in the classic movie *Au Hazard Balthazar*. Ms. Green says that her father "hated the whole experience. You can see it in the film. He has two scenes—he's sitting on a bench, and he looks so bored. [Director Robert] Bresson could be very precise, very specific, and he was quite hard on my father. My father was like, 'I'm a dentist. I don't want to be an actor anyway. Why are you shouting at me?'"[5]

• Here are some Henry Irving anecdotes: 1) The great actress Ellen Terry once said that if she were to die, her co-star, Sir Henry Irving, would say, "What a pity," pause, and then ask, "Who is there—er—to go on for her tonight?" 2) A reporter once asked the great 19th-century actor Sir Henry Irving, "To what do you attribute your success?" Sir Henry replied, "To my acting." 3) Sir Henry Irving faced a problem when he wanted to play Napoleon, a short man—he was too tall to play him. Sir Henry solved the problem by having the stage props built oversize and by appearing on stage in the company of men who were very tall. 4) The great 19th-century actor Sir Henry Irving was a generous employer. When he hired Jessie Millward, he found out that she had been making £5 a week. He said that he couldn't pay her that amount, and she was disappointed—until he said that he would pay her £12 a week for the first year and £16 a week for the following year.[6]

• Actor Brian Blessed is respectful of courage. He played Banquo to Peter O'Toole's Macbeth in 1980, and he says that the critics "eviscerated" Mr. O'Toole, who was very aware of and very affected by what they were saying and writing about him. At one point shortly before the play closed, Mr. Blessed saw Mr. O'Toole in his dressing room, emotionally in pain and "on his knees, screaming like a banshee, destroyed in heart and soul." Mr. Blessed told him, "F**k it, Peter," believing as he did that "the audience were only coming to see him suffer." Mr. O'Toole, however, replied, "No—I'll go on." Mr. Blessed says, "I have never—never!—seen courage like that. My dad, who once saved 300 lives down the [coal-mining] pit, said he knew of no one who had the courage O'Toole displayed that evening."[7]

• Artist James Montgomery Flagg was a friend of the Barrymores, whom he greatly respected and liked. He remembers being with John "Jack" Barrymore in his dressing room after a theatrical performance. Jack was in his undershirt and was removing his makeup. Mr. Flagg remembers that some of the makeup got on Jack's undershirt, which was already stained with makeup. Mr. Flagg wrote about Jack's undershirt, "Obviously, it had not collected all that gruesome brown in a mere week." Mr. Flagg remembers that Jack did not dance. He asked him about it, and Jack replied, "Unless I could be the best god*mned dancer in the world, I wouldn't dance!" Of course, Jack had a drinking problem, but Mr. Flagg evaluated Jack in this way: "Great in spite of grog."[8]

• Benjamin Terry attempted to get his young daughter Nellie interested in acting on the stage by having her play the Spirit of the Mustard Pot. However, during rehearsals of the pantomime, she screamed and kicked whenever she was placed in the Mustard Pot. Her father was embarrassed and told her, "You'll *never* make an actress." He was wrong—young Nellie grew up to become the great actress Ellen

Terry. In 1925, when she was 77 years old, actress Ellen Terry became a Dame of the British Empire. King George V performed the private ceremony in the Throne Room, following which Ms. Terry turned around and walked out, and then exclaimed, "Oh, dear! I quite forgot to walk out backward!" King George V laughed.[9]

• Sir Ralph Richardson once starred as Macbeth in a critically savaged production. The morning after opening night, his colleague Raymond Westwell arrived at the theater at the same time as he to pick up his mail. Mr. Westwell didn't speak to him, either because he didn't see him or because he was too embarrassed to say anything after reading the critical notices. After the second performance, Sir Ralph Richardson joked to him, "You cut me this morning. If you do it again, I shall bruit it about that you were seen playing Banquo to my Macbeth."[10]

• O. Smith, nee Richard John Smith, acquired his nickname because of his performance as the malevolent Obi, or Three-Fingered Jack. A 19th-century actor, he was the Boris Karloff of his day—menacing onstage, but gentle offstage—and he was so popular that if his troupe wanted to produce a play that did not contain a malevolent character for him to act, one had to be created. For example, when his troupe played John Buckstone's *Last Days of Pompeii*, the character of the Witch of Vesuvius was created especially for him.[11]

• Some actors and actresses refuse to miss a performance. One such actress was Ethel Merman, about whom it was said that if you wanted to vanish from show business, the best way was to be her understudy. Why? She once said, "I'm gonna take a chance on some young cutie going out there and being better than me? Fat chance!" (Actually, she used stronger language than that.) One of Dick Cavett's friends was Ms. Merman's understudy in *Call Me Madam*. This understudy was told, "If a cement truck hits Ethel, she goes on."[12]

• Eli Wallach once auditioned for the part of the soothsayer in William Shakespeare's *Antony and Cleopatra*. He had said perhaps six lines when the man auditioning him, Guthrie McClintic, said, "I'll read the part of Antony," and then performed a long monologue while Mr. Wallach listened. Mr. McClintic then said, "That was a wonderful scene. Good! That was good. Yup, you've got the part." Mr. Wallach reflected, "It pays to listen."[13]

• Edwin Forrest (1806-1872) was immensely proud of his performances as King Lear. A friend once complimented him: "Mr. Forrest, I never saw you play Lear as well as you did last night." The compliment, however, made Mr. Forrest angry. He responded, "*Play* Lear! What do you mean, sir? I do not *play* Lear. I play Hamlet, Richard, Shylock, Virginius, but by God, sir, I *am* Lear!"[14]

• Alexander Woollcott was a sometime actor, and after playing the Sheridan Whiteside character in *The Man Who Came to Dinner*, he made a curtain speech in which he said, "It's not true that the role of the obnoxious Sheridan Whiteside was patterned after me. Whiteside is merely a composite of the better qualities of the play's two authors." [15]

• Paul, Joe, Mark, and Stephen McGann are all brothers, and they are all actors. Constantly, each of them is mistaken for one of his brothers. Paul points out an advantage of these cases of mistaken identity: "I can always say, 'Thank you, so glad you liked it.' Or if they didn't like it, I can say, 'Oh, that was Stephen, actually.'"[16]

• At first, Zero Mostel wasn't interested in the script that later became *Fiddler on the Roof*. Walter Matthau read for the part instead, and told the producers, "You know who you should get to play this part, don't you? Zero!" The producers told him, "If we could get Zero, do you think you'd be reading for it?"[17]

• John Barrymore was playing Richard III when someone laughed as he declaimed, "A horse, a horse! My kingdom for a horse!" Mr. Barrymore pointed to the section of the theater where the laugh had come from and said, "Make haste and saddle yonder braying ass!"[18]

• Actress Coral Browne once performed in a production of *Oedipus Rex* that featured a 19-foot-long golden phallus. When she was asked what she thought of it, she replied, "Well, it's no one I know."[19]

• When the fortyish great actress Jane Cowl was criticized for appearing on stage as Shakespeare's 14-year-old Juliet, she replied, "You have to be forty to understand the wonder of being fourteen."[20]

• Theatrical director George Abbott detested Method acting. A young Method actor once asked him, "What is my motivation?" Mr. Abbott replied, "Your job."[21]

• When British character actress Margaret Rutherford was made a Dame of the Order of the British Empire, she commented, "I'd better pull my socks up."[22]

Advice

• Fay Kanin wrote a play titled *Goodbye, My Fancy*. Max Gordon, a man who had produced the hit *Born Yesterday*, read and liked the play, but in a meeting with Ms. Kanin, he pointed out that he could produce one more play that season. He also said that he had to choose between two plays. One play was by the hit-making team George S. Kaufman and Edna Ferber, and the other was by Fay Kanin, an unknown. He then asked Ms. Kanin, "Now if you were me, which would you choose?" Ms. Kanin was honest, and she said that she would choose the play by Mr. Kaufman and Ms. Ferber. Mr. Gordon did produce that play, and it closed quickly. Ms. Kanin and her husband produced her play, even though they had to get a bigger mortgage on their house to do so. *Goodbye, My Fancy* turned out to be a big hit. One day, Mr. Gordon attended the play and then said to Ms. Kanin, "Why did you have to give me such lousy advice?"[23]

• Sacha Guitry was a great French theater and film actor. Once a young USAmerican woman asked him to hear her recite and then give her advice. Mr. Guitry agreed, listened to the woman, and then kissed her on the cheek and advised her, "My dear child, marry soon. Goodbye."[24]

Alcohol

• British actor Leslie Banks was at a cocktail party where an inebriated gentleman complained that Mr. Banks wasn't drinking. Mr. Banks replied that he had had one drink and that was enough until he'd finished working that night. "Working at this time of night?" the gentleman asked. "What do you do?" After Mr. Banks had explained that he was an actor, the gentleman replied, "Oh yes, better not have a drink. You've got to be careful. It would never do if you went down to the theater and put on the wrong disguise."[25]

• Theater critic Michael Billington once enjoyed a lunch with lots of alcoholic refreshments with a Polish critic, and then he left to review a performance of Chekhov's *Three Sisters*. However, when he arrived at the theater he noticed that the theater was spinning. He also noticed that the number of sisters seemed to multiply—at one point, he counted 27 sisters! Mr. Billington says, "I fled, guilty and ashamed, and vowed never to drink on the job again."[26]

• Irish playwright Brendan Behan got drunk and then attended a performance of one of his plays, where he was very rowdy and shouted things at the cast, such as, "Why don't you do the play properly?" (The cast yelled back at him, "Why don't you shut up?") The stage manager told the audience, "How can I throw him out? He's the author."[27]

• Columnist Lucy Mangan's father once delivered a script to the house of the great actor Sir Ralph Richardson, who asked him in for a drink. Sir Ralph got a bottle of gin and said, "This is for you." He got another bottle and said, "This is for me." Then he got a bottle of tonic and said, "We'll share this."[28]

Animals

• Ermines are weasels with white fur that live in the Arctic. Their valuable fur is much sought after by hunters, who trap them by placing salt on the ice. The ermine's tongue freezes to the ice when it licks the salt. Actor Laurence Olivier read about this in a magazine, and while playing the lead in a 1945 London production of *Oedipus the King*, he used the effect it had on him to help him produce a bloodcurdling scream.[29]

• Opera singer Luigi Ravelli regarded his dog as his best critic. Before a performance, he would sing to his dog. If his dog wagged its tail, he would perform happily on stage, but if his dog growled, he would perform unhappily—and would not give his best performance. [30]

Art

• Rocker Alice Cooper has had some strange experiences. In 1973, he worked with surrealist artist Salvador Dalí, who made a rotating hologram of Mr. Cooper's head, which (the hologram, not the actual head) is now in the Dalí Museum in St. Petersburg, Florida. According to Mr. Cooper, Dalí was "the strangest thing. I'm pretty sure there are aliens that walk among us. And it's always the guys who are in first place. The guy in first place is way, way ahead of the guy in second place. The Beatles, for instance — the next band down was way, way down. And that's Salvador Dalí." The great artist knew how to make an entrance. Mr. Cooper remembers, "First of all nine nymphs walk in. Then Gala [Mr. Dalí's wife] walks in — she's in a full tuxedo and spats, white gloves, the whole lot. Then in comes 'the Dalí.' 'The Dalí is here.' He's got a giraffe-skin coat on, blue velvet pants and a pair of Aladdin shoes. He sits down and orders everyone a Scorpion, which is a shell full of every alcohol you can think of, with an orchid floating in it." So what was it like to work with the great surrealist? Mr. Cooper remembers, "He'd say one word in Portuguese, one word in French, then one word in Italian, as well as some weird surrealistic language. We worked with him for three days [and] then afterwards, at a press conference, a journalist asked me the same thing. I told them, 'It was great, but I didn't understand a word he said!' Then Dalí goes, 'Perfect! Confusion is the greatest form of communication!' And I look at him and I go, 'You speak ENGLISH? After three days of BABBLING?' By the way, Mr. Cooper was asked to run for Governor of Arizona in the

1980s, but he declined the offer. He remembers, "I told them I didn't have enough indictments. I wasn't crooked enough to be a politician. I told them, 'I can't take the pay cut!' Also, it would have killed my golf game."[31]

Audiences

• Carl Reiner wrote a funny play titled *Something Different* that lasted three months on Broadway, which is good, but Mr. Reiner had hoped for a longer run. Still, he got some ego-boosters from the run, such as the time a little old man ran on stage at the end of a performance. The little old man was Groucho Marx, who asked the audience if the play was the funniest thing that they had ever in their lives seen. The audience said that it was, and Groucho told the audience members that they had the responsibility to keep the play on Broadway by giving it positive publicity through word of mouth. Another ego-booster came when actress Joan Hackett attended a performance while wearing leotards because she went to the theater directly after dance class. She said to Mr. Reiner that she found the play so funny that "I peed in my leotards and couldn't stop! I sat through the whole show with water squishing in my Capezios." A third ego-booster occurred when a British man showed him a scar on his forehead and said, "Somewhere in the first act, when the heavyset black woman and the author are discussing his play, I found her critique of Bud's play to be so uproariously funny that I burst out laughing. Involuntarily, to be sure, my head flew forward and I gashed my forehead on the seat in front of me. I bled like a stuck pig." For the rest of the play, he held a handkerchief to his forehead. After the play, he saw a doctor and got a stitch or two.[32]

• Some audiences are more difficult than others. Barry Sullivan (1821-1891) once had the misfortune to play Hamlet before an audience in which were many drunken British soldiers. As he started reciting the "To be or not to be" soliloquy, one of the drunken sailors shouted, "Barry, give us a hornpipe [dance]." Mr. Sullivan scowled at the interrupter and then resumed the soliloquy, only to be interrupted by another request for a hornpipe. This time, he advanced to the footlights, gave a lecture to the interrupter, then again resumed the soliloquy—only to be interrupted yet again by a request: "Barry, are you going to give me and my friends a hornpipe or am I to come down and make you?" Hearing this, and laughing, Mr. Sullivan said, "Gentlemen, as you insist upon my performing a Sailor's Hornpipe in the midst of this sublime tragedy, I will even do so." He danced a very good Sailor's Hornpipe and then resumed the role of Hamlet without further interruption.[33]

• In 1842, Franz Liszt played some concerts in Berlin. He realized that many of the university students in that city were impoverished, so he scheduled a student concert for which the tickets were sold at a very low price. Unfortunately, the university professors considered themselves invited to the concert, and they bought so many tickets for themselves, their families, and their friends that few if any students could attend the concert. Liszt noticed this and was made unhappy by it, but he performed as usual. After the concert, Liszt met some students and promised them a concert for students only—no professors allowed. He kept his promise, and a few days after the students-only concert, he took 800 students to a near-by castle for a lunch that was provided by a wealthy friend. At the lunch, Liszt made a speech and said to the students, "If at any time any of you meets me anywhere, he is my invited guest."[34]

• Once, Margot Fonteyn and Rudolf Nureyev were scheduled to dance the *Corsair* pas de deux for 10 minutes; however, Ms. Fonteyn was unhappy because intermissions had been scheduled before and after their dance, and she worried that the audience would feel cheated with only 10 minutes of dancing. Frederick Ashton told her, "It will be all right. Ten minutes of *Corsair* and twenty minutes of applause. What are you worrying about?" The performance and the applause went exactly as Mr. Ashton had foretold they would.[35]

• William H. Crane, an actor of the early 20th century, told a story about long-haired playwright Al Travers, who put on a play in a theater in Savannah, Georgia. Unfortunately, the play failed—miserably. Mr. Travers sat in the front row listening to hisses from the audience. A woman behind him leaned forward and said to him, "Pardon me, sir, but knowing you to be the author of this play, I took the liberty, at the beginning of the performance, of snipping off a lock of your lock. Allow me to return it."[36]

• The pianist Vladimir de Pachmann was once disappointed with the audience's reaction to his performance at a concert, so he threatened not to finish the concert because he was not appreciated. His manager begged him to continue, pointing out that he always appreciated his playing. Therefore, Mr. de Pachmann seated his manager on the stage, and after performing each piece, he stood up, ignored the audience, turned to his manager, and bowed.[37]

• At the end of *Hamlet*, a very long play, everyone—both the audience and the actors—are tired. Near the end of the play, the great actor John Gielgud recited the lines, "If it be now, 'tis not to come; if it be not to come, it will be now." Unfortunately, the references to time reminded a man in the front row that he needed to wind his watch, which he proceeded to do very loudly. Mr. Gielgud found it very difficult to finish the play.[38]

• Ron Athey, the controversial performance artist, remembers as his favorite performance experience a blood-soaked piece that had members of the audience literally screaming. After the performance, he discovered that so many members of the audience had fainted that they had to be drug out of the nightclub onto the sidewalk despite a rainy night.[39]

• At a 1900 performance of Shakespeare's *Pericles*, a critic sat near two women, one of whom had a copy of the play and attempted to follow the action on stage with the words in the book. Finally she gave up and told her friend, "The play on the stage seems to be quite different from the book."[40]

• Audiences are important. After Oscar Wilde had written *The Importance of Being Earnest* and before it had premiered, someone said to him, "Oscar, I hope the show is a success." Mr. Wilde replied, "The show is already a success. I hope the audience is."[41]

• Pia Zadora once played the role of Anne Frank very badly. How badly? In the scene where the Nazis arrive to take the Frank family out of hiding and to the concentration camps, the audience yelled, "She's upstairs!" (This story is apocryphal—but funny.)[42]

• Peter Dews directed a production of *Antony and Cleopatra* at Chichester in 1969. After one performance, he overheard one woman audience member say to another, "Yes, and the funny thing is, *exactly* the same thing happened to Monica."[43]

• Entertainers use different methods to get themselves up for a performance. Comedian Jay Sankey once saw a magician jumping up and down in a bathroom, saying, "I love my audience! I love my audience!"[44]

Autographs

• During their 22-year touring career, and later, the Ramones signed many, many autographs, and they even once autographed a human skull. Lead singer Joey Ramone remembers perhaps the most unusual object they signed: "In Europe, one fan pulled off his artificial leg and had us sign the prosthesis." While the Ramones were at an airport in Argentina, the guards stopped them as they were going through the metal detectors, in order to get their autographs. After the band finally broke up, guitarist Johnny Ramone became a huge collector of celebrities' autographs. He used to write celebrities and say, "I am Johnny Ramone—can you please send me an autograph? I would like to add it to my collection." Many celebs responded favorably.[45]

Bathrooms

• Actress Tallulah Bankhead frequently did not bother to close the door while she was in the bathroom. Shortly after a Los Angeles newspaper had published a feature article titled "The Exotic of Exotics" about Ms. Bankhead, she was in a bathroom at her film studio when a writer walked through the open door, saw her sitting on the toilet, and said, "Good morning, Exotic of Exotics."[46]

• The Globe, which presented plays by part-owner William Shakespeare, lacked bathrooms. Outside the theater, by the banks of the Thames, stood a row of outhouses. Inside the theater, some patrons may have used slop buckets to relieve themselves during the three hours or so it took to watch a play.[47]

Chapter 2: From Children to Dance

Children

• Drama critic Alexander Woollcott was an original. Often, his small nieces visited him, and he sent them in the company of one of his friends to see a play that he had selected for them to see. Often, the play was about adult themes, which did not bother the young nieces, although shocked playgoers sometimes reprimanded Alec's friend for allowing such young girls to see such a play. By the way, his nieces discovered that in Alec's bathroom was a portrait of him sitting on the toilet and reading. Alec could be humorously blunt. Whenever his nieces would leave after the weekend, he would tell them, "I'm sick of having you around. Now get the hell out of here." And when Polly, his youngest niece, achieved age 14 and finally wore a grown-up outfit, he displayed her to his friends and announced, "This is my niece Polly, who is going to be a prostitute."[48]

• Child actors in theater sometimes do things that they are not allowed to do at home—for example, use profanity. Matilda, the young daughter of Jackie Castrey, said the word "f**k" while performing in the play *The City*, something for which Jackie was criticized in a review. However, Jackie defended herself by saying, "It's not something you go into lightly. We read the script before the auditions. When she was learning the lines at home, we would miss out the swear word: she knew she was only allowed to say it on stage."[49]

• When playwright Lillian Hellman was a child, she discovered that her father was having an affair, despite still being married to her mother. She was so upset that she went home, climbed her favorite fig tree, and threw herself to the ground, breaking her nose. By the way, she was bored attending Wadleigh High School in Manhattan and claimed later that she had spent much of her time there using a dictionary to look up "naughty words."[50]

• George Bernard Shaw was friends with a little girl who always greeted him with a kiss and called him "Uncle." He was away from the little girl's family for a while, during which time he grew his famous beard. When he saw the family again, the little girl did not kiss him. Her mother asked, "Dear, why don't you give Uncle a kiss?" The little girl replied, "I don't see a place."[51]

• For a while, the greatest fan of French mime Marcel Marceau was Michel, his seven-year-old son. After each performance by his father, Michel would call out, "Bravo, Papa, bravo!" His father told him repeatedly not to do that, but his son's shout secretly pleased him.[52]

Choreographers

• Here are some Léonide Massine stories: 1) Choreographer Léonide Massine once endured a train wreck in which a sleeping Englishman was doused by a bottle of mineral water that fell on him when the train derailed. The Englishman woke up and asked, "I say, could there be a leak?" 2) Choreographer Léonide Massine's brother Gregori was supposed to be studying at a school of Engineering; however, his parents eventually found out that he had not attended classes for several months, although he left his parents' home at the same time each morning and returned at the same time each evening. Instead of attending classes, Gregori had been spending the day with his girlfriend. After being thrown out of the house, Gregori joined the army, started studying again, and became a military engineer. 3) Mr. Massine once choreographed a dance with the title "*Ya s komarisom pliasala*," which means "I danced with a mosquito."[53]

Christmas

• One Christmas day, the Marx Brothers were performing in vaudeville and so they had to work on the holiday. (Being Jewish, they probably didn't mind.) They were living in a boarding house that had rooms for permanent boarders as well as rooms for temporary boarders such as vaudevillians. The boarding house had a reputation for serving good food, and the Marx Brothers and their mother, who served as their manager, were looking forward to holiday turkey, which they could smell cooking. Unfortunately, at Christmas dinner they were served baked mackerel, and they realized that the turkey was for the permanent boarders, who ate in a different dining room. They ate mackerel, but they felt bitter, and that night, after they had performed their act and everyone else had gone to bed, they broke into the kitchen and feasted on turkey leftovers as they enjoyed a belated holiday dinner. [54]

Comedians

• Here are some Beatrice Lillie stories: When Beatrice Lillie was preparing to star as Auntie Mame in the London production, she was asked if she would mind taking over for a few weeks for Greer Garson, who was starring as Auntie Mame in the New York production. Ms. Lillie said, "Of course not, dear. We always open in the provinces." 2) Ms. Lillie, aka Lady Peel, once visited John Gielgud and asked that the doorman say to him that "Her Ladyship" wished to visit. When she came in to see him, Mr. Gielgud said, "Oh, it's you! I wasn't sure whether it was Peggy Ashcroft [Dame Edith Emily 'Peggy' Ashcroft] or Noël Coward [a gay man]." 3) Ms. Lillie once saw Mary Martin of *Peter Pan* fame at the glove counter in Saks. Ms. Lillie nodded toward two very young children who were staring at Ms. Martin, and Ms. Martin said, "I know. They think I am going to fly." 4) Comedian Beatrice Lillie created a joke that was occasionally repeated by other entertainers. As the curtain raised on stage, she was discovered wearing a long evening gown. She sang a long, serious song, and then she lifted up her skirt and roller skated off the stage. 5) When a waiter spilled soup on her designer dress at a dinner party, comedian Beatrice Lillie told him, "Never darken my Dior again."[55]

• A joke that has a big build-up must have a big punchline. Will Rogers once listened to a joke with a big build-up but a small punchline and then said, "That porch is too big for the house."[56]

Concerts

• In 1958, country musician Johnny Cash performed a concert at San Quentin Prison. Years later, fellow country musician Merle Haggard told Mr. Cash that he had been at that concert. Mr. Cash said that he did not remember Mr. Haggard performing, and Mr. Haggard replied, "I was in the audience, Johnny." He had been serving three years for armed robbery and for escaping from jail. Mr. Haggard said about Mr. Cash's music, "This was somebody singing a song about your personal life. Even the people who weren't fans of Johnny Cash — it was a mixture of people, all races — were fans by the end of the show." After hearing Mr. Cash's concert, Mr. Haggard began playing with the prison's country band and eventually became a country music superstar. [57]

• George S. Kaufman once saw Marc Connelly coming from a concert by Jascha Heifetz and asked how he had liked it. Mr. Connelly shrugged and then said, "It was all right, I suppose, if you happen to like absolutely superb performances."[58]

Costumes

• Alicia Markova insisted on clean costumes, even as a very young dancer. While she was a teenage dancer for Sergei Diaghilev, she was asked to wear a costume previously worn by Vera Savina, who was wearing it when she cut her arm badly on jewels worn by her dancing partner, Léonide Massine. The costume had been cleaned, but a slight blood stain remained, which horrified Alicia. Although the blood stain would not have been visible to the audience, Mr. Diaghilev respected young Alicia's wishes and had a new costume made. While dancing in Nairobi, Ms. Markova had to keep a cat in her dressing room to catch all the mice and keep them from living in her costume baskets. For a while, she had a pet cat she named Tutu. According to Ms. Markova, Tutu was "a ballet cat because he has white back legs which make him look as if he is wearing white tights in readiness for a performance of *Les Sylphides*."[59]

• USAmerican dance pioneer Ted Shawn suffered for his art. He wore body paint that itched when he sweated and headdresses that were extremely tight so they would stay on when he danced. Of course, he looked very different off stage. Once, he heard a woman say to a friend, "Look, there goes Ted Shawn!" The second woman eagerly looked and then said with disappointment, "That's *Shawn*? Well, all I can say is, distance certainly lends enchantment." By the way, on the Japanese stage, men used to perform the roles of females. Onoe Baiko once told Mr. Shawn that his favorite roles on the stage were "ghosts, demons, and hysterical females."[60]

• Anthony Dowell both danced ballet and designed costumes, so he appreciated a good costume when he saw it. For example, while performing in *Other Dances* he wore a costume designed by Santo Loquasto. The costume was made to resemble three pieces of clothing—tights, a waistcoat, and a shirt—but it was made of one piece of spandex, which meant it stayed in place. Cleaning was easy—the costume was just thrown in a washing machine.[61]

• While dancing for the Harkness Ballet, Jimmy Dunne once was required to wear a veil attached to the mask that was part of his costume. The choreographer wanted more color to the veil, so it was painted without anyone notifying Mr. Dunne. Unfortunately, it's impossible to see through a veil that has been painted, so midway through the dance Mr. Dunne was forced to rip it off his face.[62]

• An automobile accident once left Ted Shawn and his dancers without costumes at show time. They went into a store in a small town and purchased the only thing that looked like a suitable replacement—gray jersey basketball trunks. Unfortunately, at the performance that night all of the dancers jumped into the air—and their trunks split open at the crotch.[63]

• The French actor Françoise-Joseph Talma pioneered the use of realistic costumes, including togas, in historical plays; however, some other actors resisted this change in costumes. One actor refused to wear a toga until two pockets were sewn in it in back: one pocket was for his handkerchief, and the other was for his snuffbox.[64]

Critics

• Joan Oliver Goldsmith, a volunteer singer in a chorus, does an activity she calls conductor watching. One of the conductors she watched was Robert Shaw, who told the chorus, "Every time you do a concert like this, you're placing a vote for the human spirit." According to Ms. Goldsmith, Mr. Shaw "literally embodied the essential dynamic of precision and passion — the yin/yang — that lies at the heart of music making." She asked her friend Liz about Mr. Shaw and what she loved the most about his conducting. Liz replied, "His elbows. I could get everything I needed just by watching his elbows." According to Ms. Goldsmith, "We probably could have seen the music in his kneecaps if he'd been wearing shorts." Ms. Goldsmith is also a writer, and she wrote about Mr. Shaw for the *St. Paul Pioneer Press* (Minnesota). (According to Ms. Goldsmith, "Twin Cities critics often ignore choruses to the point of pathology. How can a critic review [Handel's] *Messiah* and not mention the chorus till the penultimate paragraph?") When she mentioned the article to Mr. Shaw, he said, "Thank you for writing the article, but I never read that stuff. My secretary, Miss Frink, is collecting all the articles in a book, and I'm going to read it when I'm dead."[65]

• Here are some stories about critics: 1) Carl Sandburg was once asked by a playwright to watch his play and then comment on it; however, he fell asleep during the play. Afterward, the playwright asked, "How could you fall asleep when you knew how much I wanted your opinion?" Mr. Sandburg replied, "Young man, sleep is an opinion." 2) Critic George Jean Nathan was often cursed by theatrical producers, but he gave as good as he got, Once, he was asked whether he had been called a "pinhead" by a particular Broadway producer. He replied, "Impossible. 'Pinhead' is a word of two syllables." 3) Critic James Agate once watched a musical in which a character said, "Methinks you did wrong to come." Mr. Agate left the theater, saying later, "Methought this was addressed to me. Metook the hint." 4) George Jean Nathan once wrote about a performance of *Uncle Tom's Cabin*: "The dogs were poorly supported by the cast." 5) Walter Winchell once said about critic Alexander Woollcott, "He always praises the first production of each season, being reluctant to stone the first cast." 6) Anthony Hope disliked the play *Peter Pan*. After watching it, he said, "Oh, for an hour of Herod."[66]

• Yiddish actor Fyvush Finkel worked both in Yiddish theater and in mainstream theater. When he was doing Yiddish theater, a critic who hated him wrote that he should stop being an actor and instead become a circus clown. This made Mr. Finkel angry, so he decided to visit the critic and let his feeling be known—physically. However, to get to the critic's office, he had to pass his father's store. His father saw him and called him into the store. His father said, "I know where you're going. You're gonna hit him, aren't you?" Mr. Finkel acknowledged the fact. However, his father advised him, "You'll make a big man out of him—leave it alone. Tomorrow people will forget about it—the audience loves you. Come, stay, have coffee." They had coffee, and his father thought for a moment, then said, "And then again, y'know—a clown in the circus is a good, steady job!" Mr. Finkel became known as "Fyvush Finkel—a face that launched a thousand shticks!"[67]

• Here are some stories about reviews: 1) Alexander Woollcott once wrote an enthusiastic review for a certain production of *Ruddigore*. Another company that was producing *Ruddigore* on tour in Georgia—completely unaffiliated with the one Mr. Woollcott had reviewed—used his review to advertise their production. This led several people in Georgia to write nasty letters to Mr. Woollcott. 2) Occasionally, a producer of a play that has been lambasted by the critics will write a sarcastic advertisement. For example, George C. Tyler once had printed in newspapers this announcement: "The notoriously bad actor, George Arliss, in a new play on that hackneyed theme, Americanism, 'Poldekin,' by the well-known hack-writer Booth

Tarkington." 3) Alexander Woollcott once wrote an enthusiastic article about a George M. Cohan revue, but said the revue was "of, by, and for Broadway" and would *not* do well outside of Broadway. The producers of the revue reproduced the article and sent it out across the United States—but omitted the word "not."[68]

• Theater critics can be vicious. While playwright Charles MacArthur was going to the opening of his play *Johnny on the Spot*, he saw a newspaper with the headline "Strafe MacArthur" above an article about Douglas MacArthur and the Japanese assault on the Philippines. He bought a copy of the newspaper, and as he passed George Jean Nathan he carried the newspaper in such a way that the famous critic saw the headline. The next day the critics really did strafe Charles MacArthur. According to Mr. MacArthur's wife, actress Helen Hayes, "He suddenly put his head against mine—and wept."[69]

• Heywood Broun was a drama critic in New York City. (He also helped start the American Newspaper Guild.) In one review, Mr. Broun called the actor Geoffrey Steyne the worst actor on the New York stage. The next time Mr. Steyne appeared in a play, Mr. Broun wrote, "Mr. Steyne's performance was not up to its usual standard." Mr. Broun was known as a social reformer as well as a writer. Once he arrived late to a dinner at the home of Averell Harriman, but excused himself by saying, "I was down in the kitchen trying to convince your butler to strike for higher wages."[70]

• Alfred Bloomingdale, famous for his department store, once produced a play on Broadway. Like so many people before and after him, he ran into out-of-town play trouble and called for George S. Kaufman, the great play doctor. Mr. Bloomingdale brought Mr. Kaufman to the play in a limousine, and after Mr. Kaufman had seen the play, Mr. Bloomingdale said to him, "Well, George, you've seen my show. Please, help me! I've put an awful lot of money into this show. What should I do?" Mr. Kaufman relied, "Close the show and keep the store open nights."[71]

• Here are two W.S. Gilbert stories: 1) William *Schwenck* Gilbert disliked Herbert Beerbohm Tree's performance of Hamlet. In a letter he wrote that it would be easy to find out who had written the plays attributed to William Shakespeare: Simply dig up the bodies of Shakespeare and Francis Bacon, and then have Tree recite Hamlet. Whichever body turns over belongs to the person who wrote the play. 2) W.S. Gilbert once made actress Henrietta Hodson very angry after she fell down on stage. He told her, "I always thought you would make an impression on the stage one day."[72]

• Robin de la Condamine was the real name of the professional actor Robert Farquharson. When John Gielgud was 19 years old, he gave a performance of Romeo that he later called "extremely immature." However, Mr. Farquharson came backstage and told him, "You have taught me something about the part of Romeo I never knew before!" Mr. Gielgud took this as a compliment and was flattered, but later a mutual friend told him, "Robin said it was the first time he had ever realized that Romeo could be played as Juliet."[73]

• Theatrical guru Danny Newman is not a fan of the Method, believing as he does that its use resulted in "morose, intellectual, and inhibited thespians who could no longer be heard in the third row." A famous critic who seems to have agreed with him was Brooks Atkinson of *The New York Times*, who once told him that he enjoyed going to Yiddish Art Theater because there he could see thespians "*who were not afraid to act!*"[74]

• A delegation of women once called on Horace Greeley, founder and editor of the *New York Tribune*, to complain about his drama critic. Mr. Greeley listened to their complaints, and then he said, "I gather from what you say that everybody is talking about the *Tribune* critic's articles." They agreed with him, and Mr. Greeley said, "Well, that's just the kind of a critic I want on my newspaper. Good day."[75]

• John Chapman, drama critic for the New York *Daily News*, loved Shakespeare. He once started to attend a new production of *Henry V* at the Shakespeare theater at Stratford, Connecticut, but was surprised to see gymnasts performing on stage. Figuring that he was early for the play, he asked an usher what was being performed on stage, and he was surprised when the usher told him that the performance was *Henry V* and that it opened with gymnasts. Mr. Chapman replied, "The hell it does," and then he left the theater.[76]

• In 1849, William Charles Macready played Hamlet while on tour in America. At one town, someone must not have liked the play because after the scene with Rosencrantz and Guildenstern, he flung half the carcass of a sheep onto the stage. By the way, critic Michael Billington once wrote about a revival of a musical: "For those of you who missed it the first time, this is your golden opportunity: You can miss it again."[77]

• Robert Benchley once attended a bad play in which a telephone on an empty stage began ringing—and ringing (apparently, an actor had missed his cue). Finally, Mr. Benchley said loudly, "Won't somebody answer that? I think it's for me." The next day, a newspaper critic wrote in his review of the play, "The only amusing line in the play was spoken by Bob Benchley, who, unhappily, was not in the cast."[78]

• For many years, John Ranken Towse was a New York theatrical critic; he was not afraid to express his opinions. At one play, he put on his overcoat before the play was over and started to head for an exit. The manager of the company said to him, "You are not going, Mr. Towse? There is another act coming." Mr. Towse replied, "Yes, I know. That is why I am going."[79]

• Here are two stories about boredom: 1) The No. 1 model for anyone who values wit and intelligence is Robert Benchley. Once Mr. Benchley was bored by a Broadway play. When a telephone began ringing on an empty stage, he said, "I think that's for me," and left the theater. 2) Heywood Broun reviewed both books and plays. He used to carry a book into the theater in case he became bored by the play.[80]

• Sometimes theatrical critics and directors behave badly. James Agate once arrived late for an act of Thornton Wilder's *The Skin of Our Teeth*, starring Vivien Leigh, due to his having enjoyed the refreshments too much at a bar during intermission. As Mr. Agate staggered down the aisle, Laurence Olivier, the very annoyed director of the play, slapped him.[81]

• Actress Tallulah Bankhead and critic Alexander Woollcott were sitting together watching a pretentious revival of Maurice Maeterlinck's *Aglavane and Slysette*. On this occasion, Ms. Bankhead proved to be the critic. She whispered to Mr. Woollcott, "There is less in this than meets the eye."[82]

• After the poor critical reception given to his play *Waiting in the Wings*, Noël Coward "rebelled against the critics." Why? "When your play has been madly cheered on the first night, you hardly expect to wake up the next morning and find you have committed a major crime."[83]

• For some actors, the only good criticism is adulatory criticism. Charles Kean once read a review in a small, unimportant publication. The review rhapsodized about his acting talent. Mr. Kean remarked, "That, sir, is what I call honest criticism."[84]

Dance

• Here are some Alicia Markova anecdotes: 1) As a young girl, Alicia Markova danced for Sergey Pavlovich Diaghilev. For a long time, she wasn't allowed to attend the receptions the other members of the ballet troupe attended, but on her 18th birthday, Mr. Diaghilev asked her to come to his table in the ballroom of the hotel the troupe was staying at in Monte Carlo. There, the troupe held a small coming-of-age party for her, she drank her first glass of champagne, and afterward she was allowed to attend the receptions the other members of the troupe attended. 2) As part of her costume while dancing in *The Firebird*, Alicia Markova applied a sticky body-wash to her arms and back, then her dresser threw gold dust on her so that the gold dust would glitter as she danced. Because the gold dust was rough and would scratch her skin, she was unable to simply wipe it off, so after a performance she would put on a sweater, go out to eat with friends, then soak off the sticky body-wash and gold dust at home. 3) While dancing with the Diaghilev Ballet, young ballerinas Alicia Markova and Alexandra Danilova used to be taught privately by George Balanchine, who hummed marches for them to dance to because they didn't have a pianist. 4) Alicia Markova once danced in *Murder in Adagio*, which she believes is the first murder-mystery ballet. In it, she played a typist who uses a poisoned typewriter ribbon to murder people.[85]

• Here are some dance anecdotes: 1) At age nine, George Balanchine hoped to enroll in the Imperial Naval Academy, but he discovered that all the cadets had already been selected for the year. While in St. Petersburg, he accompanied his sister Tamara to her audition at the ballet academy of the Imperial School, where he was asked to audition, too. Tamara didn't pass the audition, but young George did. Later, he became a world-famous choreographer. By the way, as a young ballet student, he acquired the nickname "Rat" because he had a habit of showing his teeth while sniffing. 2) In 1976, Mikhail Baryshnikov danced in *Push Comes to Shove*, which Twyla Tharp had choreographed especially for him. He was very successful in the role—so successful that the American Ballet Theatre decided that if he were ever to become injured or ill, the ballet would be cancelled. No other dancer would be allowed to appear in his place. 3) Choreographer Bob Fosse greatly admired dancer Fred Astaire. Once, Mr. Fosse saw his idol kick a nail on the floor and send it flying into the air until it stuck on a wall. Mr. Fosse practiced for hours until he could perform the same stunt. 4) When Martha Graham was in her early eighties, she was asked what the future of modern dance would bring. She replied, "If I knew, I'd do it."[86]

• Here are a few dance anecdotes: 1) In Washington, D.C., the stagehands let the curtain down right in the middle of a *pas de deux* by Maria Tallchief and André Eglevsky, leaving Ms. Tallchief in front of the curtain and Mr. Eglevsky behind the curtain. Mr. Eglevsky remained calm and simply rejoined Ms. Tallchief on stage, where they bowed to the audience and called the dance *finis*. 2) The most memorable experience of George Skibine's career came after he received wonderful criticism for his dancing of Prince Sapphire in *Bluebird*: "Skibine danced with such personal radiance that he lifted the ballet to new heights of romance." Impresario Sol Hurok read this notice and immediately doubled Mr. Skibine's salary. 3) When Alicia Alonso was a little girl in Cuba attending ballet class while wearing tennis shoes—due to a shortage of ballet slippers—her teacher held up a small pair of ballet slippers and announced that they would be given to whichever student they fitted best. When young Alicia put on the slippers, they fit perfectly, and she rose to her feet, danced, and cried, "Look! Look! They fit!" 4) Early in her career as a ballet dancer, Mary Ellen Moylan's name appeared in programs as Mary Ellen, but she disliked reviewers referring to her as "Miss Ellen," so she decided to use her full name.[87]

Here are some anecdotes about dance and dancers: 1) Dancer Ted Shawn once kissed Gloria Swanson in a Cecil de Mille movie for a count of 28 seconds. For this effort, he was paid $500. When Mr. Shawn told Ethel Barrymore about the kiss, she said, "Kiss Gloria Swanson? Five hundred dollars? Ted, my dear, not half enough!" 2) Ruth St. Denis enjoyed improvising, on stage and off. For her solos, this was fine, but a company of dancers on stage needs some sense of direction. Once in a while, as Miss Ruth continued to work on and improvise a dance in rehearsal, her mother would tell her, "Ruthie, whatever you have just done, stays. No more changes." 3) At Ted Shawn's Jacob's Pillow, a dance retreat, were several cabins for women. Each of the cabins was named after a famous ballerina—Alicia Markova, Maria Tallchief, Nora Kaye, Alexandra Danilova, etc.—and each cabin contained a toe shoe autographed by that ballerina. 4)

Dance critic Walter Terry learned to respect dance physically. As a university student, he was used to taking gym class twice a day—his own class as well as a friend's; however, after his first dance class, his knees buckled under him and he fell down a flight of stairs.[88]

• Choreographer Tommy Tune said, "Never underestimate the benefits of down time." Not thinking about steps is one way to create steps when your creativity has been blocked. While working on creating movement for *The Will Rogers Follies*, Mr. Tune was blocked. People were asking him a question to which he had no answer other than "I don't know": "What do we do now?" So Mr. Tune excused himself, went into a dirty, dingy restroom, got on his knees and scrubbed the floor, and then stood up and scrubbed the sink. He then washed his hands, went back to work, and solved the problem that had been blocking him. He says, "While I was engrossed in the cleaning, my subconscious kicked in and took care of business. I have since come to realize that you can't force a creative thought. Down time will help you get there."[89]

• Here are some George Balanchine stories: 1) George Balanchine seldom used modern dance choreographers at the New York City Ballet. Although Martha Graham worked there in 1959, and Merce Cunningham worked there in 1966, Mr. Balanchine explained that they were there because they were "friends of Lincoln's"—that is, friends of Lincoln Kirstein, who originally proposed to Mr. Balanchine that he come to the United States and establish ballet here. 2) Some people criticize George Balanchine's choreography of *Union Jack* because they say that it is not like a real parade. Mr. Balanchine's answer to one such critic was, "If you want the real thing, go to Fifth Avenue," the location of many New York parades. 3) George Balanchine preferred the phrase "ballet master" to the word "choreographer." His tombstone and the tombstone of Marius Petipa, choreographer of *Swan Lake*, bear the phrase "Ballet Master." 4) George Balanchine went against custom by choreographing for tall ballerinas. He said, "I like tall. With tall you can see more; with short, you can see less."[90]

• Here are a few dance anecdotes: 1) At the 1976 International Ballet Competition held in Varna, Bulgaria, Patrick Dupond won the gold medal in the junior division and also won a special citation for technical excellence. Back in his native France, Mr. Dupond danced the usual test for promotion at the Paris Opera. Although the audience had been instructed to remain silent, it burst into applause—and Mr. Dupond was awarded the rank of coryphée. 2) Ballerina Natalia Makarova learned at the Kirov School of Ballet that the essence of a character can be found in the way she walks, and so Ms. Makarova approached characters such as Giselle, Odette, and Juliet by first figuring out the way the character ought to walk. 3) In ballet, male dancers wear makeup. Fortunately for them, often the makeup can be applied in a mere half-hour, whereas a female dancer may have to take two or three hours to apply her makeup because of the many layers—each layer must dry before the next layer can be put on.[91]

• Here are some Mr. Bojangles stories: 1) Famous dancer Bill Robinson, aka Mr. Bojangles, was performing in East St. Louis when a man in the audience started making a noise like a Bronx cheer. Mr. Bojangles stopped his act and said, "There's a fellow sitting down there that don't like me. Now what is your story?" The man made more noise, so Mr. Bojangles jumped off the stage, grabbed him, and threw him out. The audience cheered him when he returned to the stage to continue his act. 2) Mr. Bojangles was famous for his stair dance, in which he danced up and down a flight of stairs. Fred Stone, another dancer, once used the stair dance in his performance and sent Mr. Bojangles a check for $1500—"in part payment for the stair dance I stole from you." 3) When Mr. Bojangles was dying, letters and cards containing prayers for his recovery came to his family in Harlem. Many of the letters and cards were addressed simply "Bojangles, N.Y.," but they were delivered, as the senders hoped they would be.[92]

• Here are some dance anecdotes: 1) Some ballet performers create excitement. During the last night of a New York engagement of *Romeo and Juliet*, ballet partners Antoinette Sibley and Anthony Dowell were rewarded with a 25-minute ovation. Some members of the audience carried banners reading "Sibley and Dowell Forever." And one person even called ballet partners Suzanne Farrell and Peter Martins "Mr. and Ms. God." 2) One of the great dance teams of all time is Anna Pavlova and Mikhail Mordkin, but mishaps happen even to great dance teams. While touring, they performed in Mordkin's "Legend of Azyiade," based on *The Arabian Nights*. During a performance, Ms. Pavlova with her usual vigor hurled herself into Mr. Mordkin's arms, and the sofa he was sitting on collapsed. 3) Ballet partners Karen Kain and Frank Augustyn were able to lose weight very easily while performing in Russia—they didn't know how to order food in Russian restaurants. [93]

• Sometimes, bad things happen: 1) Ballerina Natalia Makarova worried about the audience at the Reggio Theatre in Turin where she was to dance *The Rite of Spring*. Before she danced, Placido Domingo, one of the world's greatest tenors, sang in *Un Ballo in Maschera*—and the La Scala audience ripped him to pieces, booing, whistling, and even throwing apples at him during his performance. Fortunately, when Ms. Makarova danced, there were no boos, no whistles, and no apples. 2) Ms. Makarova once wrote about the tight grip the communists kept on the arts in the former Soviet Union, "The Party administration which oversaw the Kirov did not understand that it is impossible to produce a ballet about the construction of a hydroelectric plant."[94]

• Here are some dance anecdotes: 1) Anton Dolin is actually an Irish dancer of ballet. His real name is Sydney Francis Patrick Chippendale Healey-Kay. And ballet dancer Maria Tallchief's real Native American name is Ki He Kah Stah Tsa. 2) Ballerina Margot Fonteyn danced in Roland Petit's *Paradise Lost*, which required her to crawl through a 30-foot passage to get to a trap door. During one performance, as she crawled along the passage, she thought to herself, "This is a hell of a way to spend your 48th birthday." 3) Early in his career, before becoming a famous dancer, Jacques d'Amboise was listed in a program for John Cranko's *Witch* as one of the two "Bald Heads." [95]

• Small details can make a big effect. Ballerina Suzanne Farrell once spent New Year's Eve in Monte Carlo where she saw a cabaret. One performer, wearing sequins and feathers, seemed as bored as the other performers, but as the spotlight hit her, she raised her eyelids and the spotlight hit her eyes, producing a magical effect. Ms. Farrell immediately told herself to remember this effect, and she used it to good effect in her performance in *Union Jack*, resulting in quite a lot of positive comment.[96]

• The father of influential dance teacher Nicolas Legat was Gustav Legat, also a dancer. The elder Legat was known for his ability to turn his feet outward to a phenomenal degree—an ability he developed in part by sleeping with his feet fixed in such a position that the insteps faced upwards. (His ability to turn out his feet to this degree did have a disadvantage—he was never able to achieve much elevation in his jumps.)[97]

Chapter 3: From Death to Media

Death

• When Rita Moreno was 13 years old, she made her Broadway debut as Angelica in the play *Skydrift*. During a preview before the play officially opened, she made a mistake because of her youth. The lead actress, Lilly Valente, was making an emotional speech but getting little reaction from the audience, so Rita, who was eating spaghetti on stage, decided to enliven the scene with comedy. For example, she held her fork above her head and then dropped the spaghetti in her mouth. Ms. Valente, of course, was furious and told Rita afterward, "If you ever, ever do that again, anywhere in the world, I will hear about it, and you will die. I'll see to it."[98]

• In the mid-1980s, Anthony Hopkins and Judi Dench performed in William Shakespeare's *Antony and Cleopatra* together. Often, actors are wary of playing Mark Antony, because he dies and the last act belongs to the actress playing Cleopatra. Mr. Hopkins, however, had been recently playing very demanding parts, so he welcomed being able to die early. As his character lay dying on stage, he would sometimes whisper to Ms. Dench, "Just think of it. In a few minutes I'm going to be in the dressing-room, having a nice cup of tea, and you've got all this rubbish to speak for the next hour."[99]

• Tom Lehrer is famous for his comic songs, but one of his lesser-known activities is that he likes to start rumors that he is dead. He even has a collection of newspaper and magazine articles that refer to him as the late Mr. Lehrer. He once said, "When I was in college, there were certain words you couldn't say in front of a girl. Now you can say them, but you can't say *girl*."[100]

• When Sir Cameron Mackintosh was a schoolboy, he already knew that he wanted to be a theatrical producer. He often made up an excuse that would get him out of school so that he could attend a play opening. He remembers his housemaster saying to him, "I hear your grandmother is terminally ill … again. What's opening?"[101]

• Theatrical actress Beatrice Lillie's son, Robert, was killed in action in Ceylon while Ms. Lillie was performing in the play *Big Top*. Feeling that the show must go on, she posted this note for her fellow actors backstage: "I know how you all feel. Don't let's talk about it. Bless you. Now let's get on with our work."[102]

• Wilson Mizner and Paul Armstrong wrote several plays together, but they frequently argued over who should get the credit for writing various parts of their plays. When Mr. Armstrong died and a minister gave his eulogy at the funeral, Mr. Mizner said, "That's the only thing Paul didn't say he wrote."[103]

• When Henrik Ibsen was lying ill in bed, he heard his doctor say that he (Ibsen) was somewhat better. Mr. Ibsen said, "On the contrary"—and died.[104]

• When asked which inscription should be put on his tombstone, Peter Ustinov suggested, "Keep off the grass."[105]

Eccentrics

• On stage, Chris Sievey was Frank Sidebottom, who wore a big papier-mâché head — later, it was made out of fiberglass — and he sang with a nasal twang that was native to Manchester, England. In the late 1980s, Jon Ronson played keyboards with the Frank Sidebottom Oh Blimey Big Band. He was friendly with Mike Doherty, who was Frank Sidebottom's drummer. One day, Mr. Doherty called him and said, "Frank's playing a show in London tonight and our keyboard player can't make it. Do you know any keyboard players?" He replied, "I can play the keyboards." Mr. Doherty shouted, "Well, you're in!" Mr. Ronson objected that he didn't know the songs, but Mr. Doherty asked, "Can you play C, F, and G?" He could, and Mr. Doherty shouted again, "Well, you're in!" Fortunately, since the songs were oompah versions of pop songs, Mr. Ronson picked them up quickly. Another thing he picked up quickly was that Mr. Sievey stayed in character as Frank whenever he wore the big papier-mâché head. He was wearing it when Mr. Ronson showed up for the sound check, and he ignored Mr. Ronson, who called him Chris, until Mr. Ronson finally said to him, "Hello, uh, Frank?" Then he yelled, "Hello!" For a long time, people were unaware of the identity of the man wearing the big papier-mâché head; sometimes, people would barge into the dressing room and ask people there, "It's you, isn't it? You're Frank, aren't you?" When they did this, they usually ignored Mr. Sievey, who was unassuming. Frank Sidebottom got a contract to record an album in the 1980s when he recorded his version of "Anarchy in the UK" and sent it to major music companies with this note: "Dear X, I'm thinking of getting into show business. Do you have any pamphlets?" Someone at EMI thought this was funny and asked to meet him. Frank and his big papier-mâché head showed up, and the EMI representative asked him, "Have you been in show business long?" Frank looked at his wristwatch and said, "Ten seconds." Frank and his band had some success in show business, and they once opened for Gary Glitter, whose roadies were extremely rude. Mr. Sievey and Frank both seethed, and Frank ignored the roadies' instructions: "You aren't allowed to use our lights. Stay away from our hydraulic stage." Frank jumped on the hydraulic stage, an action that set off smoke bombs and caused the stage to rise high in the air. The roadies ran toward Frank, who fled. Frank was able to shed his head and costume; underneath, Mr. Sievey was wearing his normal clothing. The roadies asked Mr. Sievey, "Have you seen Frank?" Mr. Sievey replied, "He went that way." The band took a wrong turn when it tried to become more like professional musicians; the audience loved the band's mistakes and lack of professionalism. Because of this wrong turn, the size of the audience got very small. At one show, no more than fifteen people showed up. In the middle of the show, someone in the audience produced a ball, the audience split into two teams, and they played ball during the rest of the show. Mr. Sievey always claimed to love the shows where absolutely everything went wrong. After this show, he said, "That was the best show ever." For a while Chris Evans was the driver for the band. As the driver, he said the funniest thing that Mr. Ronson has ever heard. Driving to a show, Mr. Evans stopped the car and asked a pedestrian, "Is this London?" "Yes." "Well, where do you want this wood?" The movie *Frank*, which was co-written by Mr. Ronson and Peter Straughan and stars Michael Fassbender, is based largely on Mr. Ronson's experiences in the band. [106]

Education

• Joan, the niece of drama critic Alexander Woollcott, was an activist at an early age. When she was 11 years old, she attended a school whose food was both bad and expensive. Therefore, she and her friends planned a boycott. At lunchtime, they set up three small booths and sold tasty sandwiches, cakes, cold drinks, and homemade candy at inexpensive prices. They also let their classmates know that they would not sell any treats to anyone who bought food at the school lunchroom, and so they were very successful at keeping customers out of the school lunchroom. Of course, the school principal quickly put a stop to the boycott. It seemed that Joan had lost the battle, but soon afterward the school hired a new lunchroom manager, so Joan had won after all. By the way, when Joan was in college, she was both a reporter and a dramatist. Once, she had to write an article on a drama contest in which she was taking part. Unfortunately, the deadline for the article was noon, and the winner of the drama contest would not be announced until later. When Joan was announced as the winner of the drama contest, she was happy—after all, in the article that she had already submitted to the newspaper she worked for, she had announced that she was the winner.[107]

• Alicia Markova danced on a very small stage in London at the Ballet Club. About the experience, she says, "Dancing under such intimate conditions, where one could shake hands with friends in the front row, taught me one vital lesson: all the strain and effort of dancing had to be concealed, or the illusion would be ruined. Panting and perspiration were out of the question, so I had to learn to give an impression of effortless ease and never allow my breathing to be visible from the front." Such training helped her a great deal when she danced the title role of *Giselle*, in which she played a disembodied spirit in the second half of the play—a spirit that had no need to perspire or to breathe. By the way, the great Russian dancer Lubov Tchernicheva seldom smiled when she was dancing for Sergei Diaghilev, but teenage dancer Alicia Markova knew how to cheer her up. Young Alicia would occasionally give her a bunch of carnations. Then Ms. Tchernicheva would smile.[108]

• Ruth Draper used to perform long on-stage monologues such as "The Italian Lesson," in which a New York society lady's translation of the beginning of Dante's *Inferno* is continually interrupted. Ms. Draper's monologue reveals the society lady's life. One person who was influenced by her was Joyce Grenfel, who also performed on-stage monologues. Ms. Draper was a cousin to Joyce's father, and "Miss Ruth" used to help take care of the very young Joyce and her very young brother in the nursery. Following a Ruth Draper performance in London, the adult Joyce went backstage and told her, "I don't know how anyone even dares mention my name with yours." Miss Ruth replied, "They don't."[109]

• Eli Wallach once remarked to Ernest Truex, with whom he was acting in the play *Androcles and the Lion*, "I sure got a great laugh on my last line out there." Mr. Truex asked, "*You* did?" The very next performance, Mr. Wallach said the line, waited for the laugh, and heard only silence. After the play was over, Mr. Truex explained, "You're not the only one onstage when you get *your* laugh. *Your* laugh came about because there are other actors skillfully setting up the situation for you." Mr. Wallach considers this one of his most important lessons in acting. He made peace with Mr. Truett and started getting a laugh on the line again.[110]

• When Anna Russell was attending the Royal College of Music in London, she was required to give singing concerts, at which all of the other students laughed at her. The director of the college, Sir Hugh Allan, stiffly informed her that the students were supposed to be serious about their studies. However, Ms. Russell really was serious and she sang the best she was able. Unfortunately, despite her love of opera, her voice was poor—the result of a field hockey injury to her nose, which she says ruined her "acoustics."[111]

• Garth Fagan, the choreographer of the theatrical version of *The Lion King*, learned an important lesson from Martha Graham: "Do it till you get it right!" She requested that he simply walk across the floor. He did that 12 times before he realized that she wanted a walk that did not say, "LOOK AT ME! AREN'T I GORGEOUS!" When he did the walk correctly, Ms. Graham told him, "I think you're going to go places." As the head of his own dance troupe and as a Broadway choreographer, he did.[112]

• In a school play, Peter Ustinov played one of the Sirens who attempt to lure Ulysses into sailing his ship onto rocks. Despite wearing long and golden curls, Mr. Ustinov was not an enchanting Siren. He says, "Ulysses rightly wasn't tempted. Instead, he sailed home."[113]

Fame

• While driving with his friends too fast in Regent's Park, famous actor Ralph Richardson was stopped for speeding by a police officer who didn't recognize him and so asked for identification. Sir Ralph replied, "I am Sir Ralph Richardson. Seated next to me is Sir Cedric Hardwicke and behind me is Sir Laurence Olivier." The police officer replied, "I don't care if it's the whole of King Arthur's ruddy Round Table—you're getting a summons."[114]

• Lilian Baylis was proud of her work with the Old Vic and with Sadler's Wells. One day, she was hit by a car while crossing the road with a friend. Help arrived, and the friend told them, "Don't you know who this is? This is Lilian Baylis of the Old Vic." Ms. Baylis raised herself up on one arm, said, "And of Sadler's Wells," and then fell back again.[115]

Fans

• Jazz bassist Milt Hinton was in Moscow when a Russian man approached him in the street and told him, "I am a member of the Lester Young fan club in Moscow." He then gave Mr. Hinton a button bearing a photo of Mr. Young, a famous jazz tenor saxophonist and clarinetist who was often called "Prez" by his friends. Mr. Hinton was a photographer as well as a jazz musician, and he was carrying a number of his photographs. He had a photograph of Mr. Young, and he gave it to the Lester Young fan. Mr. Hinton says, "He stared at the picture for 10 or 15 seconds, shaking his head from side to side. There were tears in his eyes. Then he grabbed me and gave me a hug. I'd never heard of a Lester Young fan club in the United States, but there I was in the middle of Moscow, hearing about a group dedicated to Prez's music. The whole scene was absolutely beautiful."[116]

• A woman once asked actress Constance Benson if she could kiss her. Because Ms. Benson felt that the kiss was desired because of her success on the stage that evening, she agreed, but after the kiss, she discovered that it was desired for another reason. During the play that evening, her character had been kissed by actor Lewis Waller, and the woman explained, "I shall never be kissed by Lewis Waller, but he has just kissed you, and that's as near to the real thing as I shall ever get." [117]

Food

• Carl Reiner once joined a group of friends who were dedicated to eating very good Chinese food and had formed an informal group for that purpose. The biggest eater among the friends was Joseph Heller, author of *Catch-22*. At a restaurant, everyone sat down, but then the friends insisted that Mr. Reiner sit in the seat of honor: the one with its back to the kitchen. This struck Mr. Reiner as odd, and he asked whether this was a tradition. Mr. Heller explained, "Traditionally, honored guests, who aren't accustomed to seeing a rat scurry across a kitchen floor, don't seem to enjoy the evening as much as those of us who are accustomed to the intrusion." When the soup was served, Mr. Heller announced, "This is a special night, and in honor of my guest, I will serve." He served himself a generous helping of soup, then gave the ladle to Mr. Reiner and said, "Now you serve." Mr. Heller had conceived an ingenious way of ensuring that he got his fair share of soup even on those occasions when perhaps not enough fair servings existed for everyone. Mr. Heller also created the touch-rice rule, which applied to everyone but himself. According to this rule, eaters had to eat a mouthful of rice after eating a mouthful of the expensive stuff from the communal dishes. Because this rule did not apply to Mr. Heller, it helped to ensure that he got his fair share of the expensive stuff. Mr. Reiner had a great time during that evening: he ate good food, he laughed long and loud with good friends, and because his back was toward the kitchen, he saw a rat only once. By the way, after the meal, Mr. Heller asked to be driven by the theater marquee that stated, "*They Bombed in New Haven: A New Play* by Joseph Heller." Looking at the marquee, he said, "Just wanted to see my name up there. I never thought I'd be on a Broadway theater marquee, and there I am! It's very exciting! Don't know how long the play will run or if I'll ever write another one, so if you guys don't mind—a couple more minutes?"[118]

• When Alexandra Danilova was a little girl, one of her aunt's suitors gave her a little wine mixed with water. She liked the taste, so the first chance she got, she switched her glass with the suitor's glass and she downed his wine. She suffered no ill effects, although she giggled a lot and felt very gay. After leaving Russia following the Revolution, ballet dancer Alexandra Danilova went to Europe, where food was plentiful and where she gained weight. At rehearsal one day, Anton Dolin complained when he had to lift her: "What do you think I am? A piano mover?" Ms. Danilova decided to lose weight, so she bought some diet pills. She read the instructions—take one pill in the morning and one pill in the evening—but she decided to take five pills immediately and lose weight more quickly. George Balanchine found her passed out on the floor, and after he found out what she had done, he threw the diet pills out the window and gave her advice about how to lose weight safely through diet and exercise. She lost the extra weight and became a ballerina.[119]

• Old Man Morris was William Morris, who started the Morris Agency. British actor Stanley Holloway acquired a deep respect for Old Man Morris after seeing what happened when Mr. Morris was handed a couple of sandwiches after missing dinner. The sandwiches were made of ham, and Mr. Morris, who was an orthodox Jew, did not eat them. Mr. Holloway thought, "Here is a man with a strong will"—something that was proven by Mr. Morris' actions as an agent.[120]

• Florenz "Flo" Ziegfeld produced many money-making spectaculars in his lifetime, but occasionally he had trouble making a decision in small matters. Songwriter Lew Brown once noticed a box of black licorice candies on Mr. Ziegfeld's desk and remarked that he didn't know that Flo liked that kind of candy. Mr. Ziegfeld replied, "I'll tell you why I eat them. They're all black, so I don't have to make up my mind which color I like best."[121]

• John Barrymore once complained when a waiter served him a lobster with one claw missing. The waiter explained, "They fight sometimes, and one loses a claw." Mr. Barrymore replied, "Then take this one back and bring me the winner."[122]

Friends

• Joan Oliver Goldsmith, a volunteer singer in a chorus, once had a dream about three friends whom she had gotten close to while carpooling to rehearsals and concerts. She told them, "I dreamt about the four of us last night. I was going somewhere very important, changing my life, leaving everything behind. They told me I could bring two treasures with me." Her friend Sandra asked, "Which two of us did you pick?" Joan replied, "I chose laughter and music. Which is just another name for you guys." By the way, Sandra, a monied woman with a successful consulting business, once said, "My ears! I forgot my earrings! I'm naked! I can't go!"[123]

Gays, Lesbians, and Transgendered People

• Richard O'Brien created *The Rocky Horror Show*, a hit on the stage. (It became the cult movie *The Rocky Horror Picture Show*.) The show features Dr. Frank N. Furter, a transvestite scientist who gives straight-couple Brad and Janet a night that changes their lives. All his life, Mr. O'Brien never felt completely male or completely female but somewhere in the middle. He does have a word to describe how he feels: transgender. He has been married twice and has children, and when he told his children that he was transgender, they said, "Dad, and your point is?" At a family gathering when his father was very elderly, his father asked him, "Richard, are there any things in your life you'd like to have changed?" Mr. O'Brien replied, "Well, I'm very grateful for the gift of life, but I think it would have made more sense if I'd been born a girl." And his father said, "I think I understand exactly what you're saying."[124]

• Singer/songwriter Levi Kreis is gay and religious, and he went through a long period of praying to be "cured" of his gayness before finally accepting it. When he had just arrived in Los Angeles, he went to see Del Shores' play *Southern Baptist Sissies*, which is about four gay boys growing up in a Baptist community. At the intermission, he was crying because, he says, "I didn't realize that my story was the story of other people. I was floored." Sitting behind him was a man who asked him if he was OK. Mr. Kreis replied, "I don't know who wrote this play, but it's just tearing me apart!" The man then said, "I wrote it. Hi. I'm Del Shores." Mr. Shores also said, "You can come back and see this play as many times as it takes you to put your past behind you." Mr. Kreis says, "I think I went to see the play 36 times!"[125]

Good Deeds

• Artist James Montgomery Flagg's father did a very good deed during the Great Blizzard of 1888 in New York, New Jersey, Connecticut, and Massachusetts, during which he got caught in the blizzard. While he was walking home, he came across a young woman who had fainted in the cold. He carried her a mile to her home and then walked the rest of his way to his home, where he used hot towels to melt the ice in his beard. (His son, young James, then eleven years old, had walked to school in snow up to his waist. When he arrived at the school, he discovered that school had been cancelled.)[126]

• Political cartoonist Herblock once drew a cartoon of President Lyndon Johnson as the Music Man, the creation of Meredith Willson, who wrote the musical *The Music Man*. Mr. Willson wrote Herblock to ask for the cartoon, and Herblock sent it to him. Mr. Willson wrote him a charming thank-you letter, and one year later, he sent him another letter saying that the cartoon was a "daily joy" and "I'd be a pig not to tell you this." Herblock said about Mr. Willson, "He must have been as charming as his songs and shows."[127]

• Actor James "Jim" Lewis was a true friend to fellow actor John Drew. A group of theatrical people and their families were staying together at West Hampton, Long Island, and Mr. Lewis saw a newspaper article in which a theatrical critic had disparaged Mr. Drew and his acting abilities (or lack of them, as the critic would have it). Mr. Lewis gathered up all the newspapers that carried the negative review in the large house the actors were staying at and cut it out of each copy so that Mr. Drew and his family would not be able to read it.[128]

Illnesses and Injuries

• What did famous actor Lionel Barrymore (who played Mr. Potter in *It's a Wonderful Life*) cut his teeth on as an infant? Possibly, but not likely, a bullet. Here's the story. While on tour in Marshall, Texas, Lionel's father, Maurice Barrymore, and another actor named Ben Porter, dined with actress Miss Ellen Cummings in a lunchroom at the Station Hotel. A man named Jim Curry, who was a deputy sheriff as well as a railroad employee, began to use foul language in front of Miss Ellen, and Maurice demanded that he stop. Jim replied, "I can do any of you up." Maurice said, "I suppose you could—with your pistol or knife." Jim said, "I haven't got any pistol or knife. I'll do it with my bunch of fives." He then displayed his fist. Maurice replied, "I'll have a go at you," and he prepared to fight. However, Jim had lied about being weaponless, and he shot both Maurice and Ben. Ben died immediately, but Maurice recovered. The town physician removed the bullet from Maurice, who said, "I'll give it to my son, Lionel, to cut his teeth on." [129]

• Tuscan tenor Galliano Masini woke up the morning of his first performance in *Aida* in Rome with a terrible feeling in his throat. Panicked, he called his physician for help. The physician looked at his throat and told him, "I'm going to spray your throat with some medicine," and then he advised Mr. Masini that if he would rest until it was time to warm up for singing that night, he would be fine. Mr. Masini followed his physician's instructions, and just as the physician had said, he sang very well that night. Later, Mr. Masini asked about the medicine the physician had sprayed on his throat, and the physician told him, "There was nothing wrong with your throat this morning. The spray I used was merely distilled water."[130]

• Suzanne Farrell, a ballerina with the New York City Ballet, suffered from arthritis late in her career. She tried many things in an attempt to cure the disease, including going to a homeopathic doctor, who had her take many minerals, including silver and gold, in an attempt to replenish her cartilage. When her husband, Paul Mejia, saw the labels on the bottles of minerals, he told her, "Honey, you're worth almost as much inside as out." The homeopathic treatment didn't work; eventually, she received a hip replacement.[131]

• Actor Jeremy Piven caused an uproar on Broadway when he stopped acting in David Mamet's *Speed-the-Plow*, alleging mercury poisoning caused by eating too much fish. Mr. Mamet came up with a cutting criticism when he said about Mr. Piven, "My understanding is that he is leaving show business to pursue a career as a thermometer." Actually, an arbitrator backed up Mr. Piven's account, but that did not stop the criticism. The tabloid *New York Post* carried a story that said, "An arbitrator bought Jeremy Piven's fish tale hook, line and sinker." [132]

Insults

• Chet Baker (1929-1988) was a jazz trumpeter and vocalist who was voted best trumpeter in the 1989 critics poll in *Downbeat Magazine* and inducted into the magazine's Hall of Fame. Actually, he was voted best trumpeter two years in a row in *Downbeat Magazine*. Mr. Baker knew that Miles Davis, a true genius, was a better trumpeter than he was, and so he told him that he felt like writing him a letter of apology. Mr. Davis told him, "You got about 15 other letters to write before you get to me." Mr. Baker could respond wittily to bad criticism when he chose to. Wynton Marsalis, who is technically superb, was critical of Mr. Baker, who was less technically accomplished but who had a distinctive and original approach to jazz. Mr. Baker responded to the criticism by saying, "If I could play like Wynton ... I wouldn't."[133]

• During a performance of Richard Wagner's *Lohengrin*, Emma Eames got the idea that Katti Senger-Battaque was trying to steal a scene from her, so she whacked Ms. Senger-Battaque on the head. After the performance, Ms. Senger-Battaque said that she wasn't upset with Ms. Eames because "I was really surprised and delighted to see any evidence of emotion in Madame Eames."[134]

• Frances Kelly, the Irish artist, once made several purchases at a London shop and then told the saleslady to send the items to the Irish Embassy. The saleslady said, "Irish Embassy? I thought you were in our Empire." Ms. Kelly replied, "Didn't know you had one."[135]

• Noël Coward wrote *Private Lives*, a comedy. Lady Diana Cooper starred in *The Miracle*, a drama. Lady Diana once told Mr. Coward,

"Didn't you write *Private Lives*? Not very funny." Mr. Coward replied, "Aren't you in *The Miracle*? Very funny indeed."[136]

• One woman of true originality and great bitchiness was Tallaluh Bankhead. After Somerset Maugham rejected her for a role in one of his plays, she told him, "Mr. Maugham, I have two words left to say to you, and the second one is 'off.'"[137]

• On the first night of a play by Oscar Wilde, an ill-wisher gave him a cabbage. Mr. Wilde responded, "Whenever I smell it, I shall be reminded of you."[138]

Language

• Jerry Orbach and his wife once attended a birthday party for Richard Burton. As a gift, they bought him a kaleidoscope. At the time, he was having an affair with a young actress named Susan Strasberg, with whom he was appearing in the play *Time Remembered*. A half-dozen women surrounded Susan and berated her for having the affair. Mr. Burton entered the room, the women grew quiet, and Mr. Burton thanked the Orbachs for their gift in a monologue with his wonderful lifting Welsh accent, mesmerizing the half-dozen women who had been berating Susan. After he left the room, Susan said to the mesmerized women, "And that's just the talk."[139]

• On 25 March 1949, the Waldorf Conference to promote peaceful coexistence between the Soviet Union and the United States opened in New York City. Magazine editor Norman Cousins spoke, but he used his time to attack the Communist Party. After he had finished speaking, playwright Lillian Hellman went to the microphone and said, "I would recommend, Mr. Cousins, that when you are invited out to dinner, you wait until you get home before you talk about your hosts." When Ms. Hellman was aged and unable to climb stairs on her own, she hired a strong UCLA student to carry her up and down the stairs of her home.[140]

• George Bernard Shaw was traveling in Italy with a group of men on a train. The train stopped at Milan, and the men got out to eat.

When it came time to leave the restaurant, they were unable to make the waiter understand that they didn't want one bill—they wanted separate bills for each of the men. Mr. Shaw thought for a while, and then he remembered a line from *The Huguenots*—"*Ognuno per se; per tutti il ciel*" (Italian for "Every man for himself, and Heaven for all"). He declaimed the line dramatically, the waiters doubled up with laughter, and Mr. Shaw soon found he had a reputation for being able to speak Italian.[141]

• Playwright Charles MacArthur and humorist Robert Benchley met at a cocktail party. Asked about the hostess by a guest, Mr. MacArthur replied, "She's too enthroned." Immediately, Mr. Benchley stepped up and said, "Very well put, sir. My name is Benchley. If you happen to be looking for a place to live, I have an apartment I'd be happy to share with you." Mr. MacArthur said, "I'm a late sleeper"—to which Mr. Benchley, another late sleeper, replied, "Delighted to hear it." Later, Mr. Benchley explained his immediate liking for Mr. MacArthur by saying, "It was the first time I heard language at a Social Party."[142]

• An actor once told playwright Sir James Barrie, author of *Peter Pan*, that without using words he could convey anything to an audience. Sir James replied, "Please express without a word that you have a younger brother, who was born in Devonshire but is now living in Kent, who is coming to London next week on Thursday to call on his sister who has sprained her ankle crossing Piccadilly as she was on her way to a Regent Street dressmaker to be fitted for a pink silk dress." [143]

• USAmericans are at a great disadvantage when it comes to laughing at opera because most of us don't know whatever language the singers are singing in. For example, in Act III of *Carmen* by the French composer Georges Bizet, the chorus of cigarette smugglers sing very loudly about how quiet they have to be because they are smugglers.[144]

• Playwright and actor Peter Ustinov had many occupations, including at one time being Rector of Dundee University. Unfortunately, he once received a letter addressed to "The Lord Rectum of Dundee University." Such an error gives one pause, and Sir Peter later said, "And that is how I have seen myself ever since in moments of self-doubt."[145]

• It is possible to be affected by a play even though you don't know the language the actors are speaking. Giacomo Puccini (1858-1924) saw a dramatization of *Madame Butterfly* in London; however, even though he didn't understand English, he was affected by the passion of the story—a story that he turned into a famous opera.[146]

• Theatrical producer Jed Harris had a well-deserved reputation for being temperamental. A sign in the reception room of his suite of offices said, "Please don't call Jed Harris a bastard."[147]

Media

• In the early part of the 20th century, a passion play was performed in Denver, Colorado. After the performance, the two actors playing Jesus and Judas Iscariot went out on the town. The two actors got drunk, and then they got in a fight, which ended when the actor playing Jesus threw the actor playing Judas through a plate glass window. Reporter Gene Lindberg wrote an article about the incident and composed this headline (which was not used): "Jesus Settles 2000-Year-Old Grudge; Knocks Judas Through Plate Glass Window." [148]

• During an actors' strike early in the 20th century, four famous theatrical producers decided to descend upon various newspaper editors in an attempt to get more favorable publicity for their side. At the *New York Times*, one of the producers told a newsboy that he wished to speak with the editor: "Will you be good enough to tell him that Mr. David Belasco, Mr. George Broadhurst, Mr. E. H. Sothern, and Mr. Harrison Grey Fiske wish to see him?" The newsboy asked, "All four of you? What do you want to do? Sing to him?"[149]

• After lesbian playwright Holly Hughes wrote *Clit Notes*, she discovered that major media avoided the word "clit." For example, the *New York Times* declined to print the title of the play, saying instead that it contained "a slang term for the word 'clitoris.'" When Ms. Hughes was interviewed on a National Public Radio station, she was told that it was OK to use the word "clitoris" when talking about herself, and she was warned not to call someone else a clitoris.[150]

Chapter 4: From Mishaps to Politics

Mishaps

• Actress Nan Martin was dancing during opening night of *The Marriage of Mr. Mississippi* at the Mark Taper Forum in Los Angeles, California, when her feet lost their footing on the steeply raked stage and she fell hard on her rear end — so hard that the stage shook and over 700 people gasped. A pro, she got up and continued dancing. At the end of her dance, the audience gave her a thunderous burst of applause. Ms. Martin reflected that the mishap is "theatre epitomized. It couldn't have happened in film or television; there would have been a re-take. But theatre is immediate, *now*, and the reality of live breathing people, flesh and blood (actors and audiences) is what makes theatre special, necessary, eternal." Here is another theatrical mishap: Actors Fritz Weaver and Albert Dekker were on stage at the Mark Taper Forum when someone in the audience sneezed. Mr. Dekker cheerfully called to the audience member, "Gesundheit!" Mr. Weaver regarded this as "an early sign that a special relationship would exist between audience and performer at the Taper." This next anecdote is not a mishap, but it is an example of the camaraderie of actors at the Taper. When deaf actress Phyllis Frelich went to the Taper to perform in *Children of a Lesser God*, most of the staff used sign language to greet her. She said that "many went well beyond 'How are you? I'm fine.' I was flattered and impressed."[151]

• Here are some Plácido Domingo anecdotes: 1) Plácido Domingo occasionally ran into a problem as he stood offstage trying to get into the proper state of mind to perform an opera. As he tried to get into the character of someone like *Otello*, people backstage would say "Ciao, Plácido" to him as if he were doing nothing important. 2) While singing in *Tosca*, Plácido Domingo has had bad luck crying out "Vittoria! Vittoria!" Once, he fell flat on his nose, creating a pool of blood; fortunately, he managed to finish the opera. On another occasion, he threw his head back as he cried "Vittoria! Vittoria!"—and broke the nose of the supernumerary standing behind him. 3) Plácido Domingo occasionally sang opera in the open air at the Cincinnati Zoo, where occasional mishaps would occur. For example, someone sang, "*Rispondimi*!" ("Answer me!), and some nearby ducks answered, "Quack! Quack!"[152]

• Annoyances do occur in the audience during live performances, and sometimes the onstage performer gets nasty and sometimes the onstage performer handles the annoyance well. In *The Iceman Cometh*, actor Tim Piggott-Smith was annoyed—make that furious—because mobile telephones kept ringing in the audience. Finally, he lost it, and he said, "If that goes off again, I'll f**king kill you." Fellow actor Kevin Spacey was less angry when that problem occurred at the Old Vic. He simply said to the audience member with the ringing telephone, "Tell them we're busy." At Edinburgh, comedian Richard Herring once threw an audience member's ringing telephone to the floor of the stage, shattering it—the telephone, not the floor. The audience members were stunned for a moment, and then they gave Mr. Herring a standing ovation.[153]

• On one occasion, Alicia Markova fractured her foot during the first act of *Giselle*, forcing her replacement in the second act by Mia Slavenska. The audience must have been startled by the substitution and by the dramatic change in Giselle's hair color, as Ms. Markova is a dark brunette and Ms. Slavenska is red-headed. And while performing the title role of *Giselle*, Ms. Markova once slipped and landed on the stage floor in an undignified position with her feet and lilies pointing straight up. Her undignified position made her laugh despite the seriousness of the role. Once, at a moment in the second act of *Giselle*, just before Giselle's main Adagio with Albrecht, everything should be absolutely silent. It was at that moment one night that Alicia Markova heard an overhead light bulb explode, showering her with fragments of glass. The rest of the performance was difficult for Igor Yousekevitch, because as Albrecht he had to fall full length on the stage floor.[154]

• While Rita Moreno was performing in Lorraine Hansberry's play *The Sign in Sidney Brustein's Window* at the Longacre Theatre in New York, a physician named Leonard Gordon asked her to a New Year's Eve party. She said yes, and she asked him to pick her up at a late hour at the Longacre Theatre. This puzzled him at first, but he thought that she must be seeing the play with a friend. He showed up as the play ended, and he waited out front. No Rita. He waited and waited, and he eventually asked a female usher to check the women's restroom. Still no Rita. Meanwhile, Rita was waiting and waiting in her dressing room. No Leonard. Finally, Leonard checked the marquee to make sure that he was at the right theater. He saw the name "Rita Moreno" on the marquee, and he then went backstage and apologized to Ms. Moreno, saying that he had not known that she was THE Rita Moreno. Later, they married.[155]

• Here are some musical mishaps: 1) Actor Harry Secombe was playing d'Artagnan in the play *The Four Musketeers* at the Theatre Royal on a hot summer matinee when some members of the audience began to fight despite the frenetic action occurring on stage. Thoroughly annoyed, Mr. Secombe ran to the footlights and screamed at the rowdies: "Do you mind keeping quiet? Some of us are trying to get some sleep up here." 2) Sir Malcolm Sargent, a world-class conductor, once made a major faux pas in front of royalty. He introduced Sergio Poliakoff to the "King of Norway," only to hear the King say, "Sweden, actually." 3) In the opera *Tosca* is a scene in which the character Scarpia attempts to rape the character Tosca. During a dress rehearsal, Norman Bailey, playing Scarpia, ran after Anne Evans, playing Tosca—and his pants fell down.[156]

• As a young man, Jerome K. Jerome (1859-1927) acted in the provinces in England, thus giving him the opportunity to be present at—and participate in—some theatrical mishaps. One theater that he and the troupe performed at had only one dressing room—which of course was given to the actresses, leaving the actors to dress on the stage, behind the curtain. At one performance, the curtain went up prematurely, revealing (carefully chosen word, that) the men dressing. Mr. Jerome, however, did not regard this incident as one of the many accidents that happen in the theater—rather, he thought it was intentionally done by a villain whose name he kept secret.[157]

• Ballerina Margot Fonteyn once was annoyed by a journalist who kept asking the same question over and over, phrased differently each time. Finally, she told him, "Tell me what answer you are trying to get, and I will tell you if I agree with it." It turned out that the journalist had a theory that the wild Tartar named Rudolf Nureyev had been tamed by dancing with her. She did not agree with this; after all, Mr. Nureyev had not been tamed by 23 years of life under Communist rule. On another occasion, some reporters became aggressive in their questioning, but she was able to make them laugh by saying, "You can read the answer to that in the papers."[158]

• After a theatrical performance by Vivien Leigh, writer Lynn Reid Banks had the task of driving Ms. Leigh to a live, on-air interview. However, Ms. Leigh refused to be hurried as she dressed, and afterward she insisted on signing a few autographs, so they did not arrive at the studio until just before the interview was scheduled, considerably rattling Ms. Banks' nerves. After the interview, Ms. Banks began venting her nerves by complaining to a friend about what a rough time she had had with Ms. Leigh—and turning around she saw Ms. Leigh's husband, Sir Laurence Olivier, who had stopped by to watch the interview.[159]

• After a performance, Anton Dolin and Anne-Marie Holmes once attended a reception given for Les Grands Ballets Canadiens dancers. However, no one came over to congratulate Ms. Holmes on her dancing or Mr. Dolin on his choreography in that evening's performance. Mr. Dolin grew angry, and he told Ms. Holmes, "Get your coat. We're leaving." She had no problem with that, so she went upstairs to get her coat. Returning downstairs, she tripped and bumped on her bottom down the steps. Mr. Dolin helped her up, and then they made a grand exit—into a closet.[160]

• Sir John Gielgud occasionally made gaffes: 1) He was in his dressing room after a theatrical performance when a man came in to see him. Sir John said, "How pleased I am to meet you. I used to know your son. We were at school together." The man replied, "I have no son—it was I who was at school with you." 2) Sir John Gielgud once saw a performance of Richard Burton in *Hamlet*, after which Mr. Burton said he was experiencing a cold. Sir John replied that he would see the play again "when you're better—in health I mean, of course."[161]

• Young, inexperienced actors sometimes get stage fright and forget their lines. Appearing with Ada Rehan was a young actor suffering from a bad case of the nerves. The actor was supposed to ask Ms. Rehan a question, and then as she hesitated, say, "You don't reply." Unfortunately, when Ms. Rehan hesitated, the actor forgot his line. A prompter from the wings of the theater whispered, "You don't reply," and the actor whispered back, "How the hell can I, when I don't know what to say?"[162]

• Dancers have to know how to act in an emergency. Alexandra Danilova was on stage dancing in *Swan Lake* one night, when a dancer offstage, Lubov Rostova, got too near a candle and caught her costume on fire. Ms. Rostova ran onstage and crossed it to get to her husband. Ms. Danilova saw that the audience was on the verge of panicking, so she continued dancing. The audience relaxed, and Ms. Rostova's costume was quickly put out.[163]

• Andrey Labinsky was a tenor who tried very hard to control his expenses. He budgeted very carefully and wrote down every cent he spent in a little book—and then he went out and lost all his money gambling. Once, he was playing poker backstage. When he went onstage, he was supposed to be carrying a large platter, but through carelessness and his hurry to meet his cue, he walked onstage carrying the poker table.[164]

• On 6 April 1759, shortly before his death, George Frideric Handel conducted his *Messiah* at Covent Gardens. One of the singers, Matthew Dubourg, didn't like to sing his part the way Handel had written it; instead, he preferred to add his own embellishments. While singing, Mr. Dubourg got off key, and it was quite a while before he got on key again. When he did, Handel shouted to the amusement of the audience, "Welcome home, Mr. Dubourg!"[165]

• A nephew of powerful theater owners Lee and Jake Shubert built the Forrest Theater in Philadelphia, but he neglected to put dressing rooms in the plans. After the theater had been built and the flaw discovered, the nephew had to buy another building at the rear of the theater to house the dressing rooms and he had to construct an underground passageway to connect the building with the theater.[166]

• Doug Gilbert, a drama critic for the New York *World-Telegram*, once had a chance to get involved in theater production. He was having dinner in a restaurant with a producer who wanted to hire him, but misfortune struck. Mr. Gilbert had ordered clam spaghetti and he had his mouth full when he suddenly sneezed—his mouth opened, and the clam spaghetti flew onto the face of the producer.[167]

• Dorothy Loudon was known as the "Queen of the Flops," because her talent graced so many plays that failed to become hits. The 1971 play *Lolita, My Love* also had a disastrous out-of-town reception. In Boston, Alan Jay Lerner, lyricist/librettist of the play, told the cast that they had to vacate the theater. Why? He said, "There's a bomb in the building." Ms. Loudon responded, "Another one?"[168]

• Lisa Kron remembers her most terrifying performance on stage well. She was working with Holly Hughes, who finished writing the piece minutes before they were to perform it. Just before they went on stage, Ms. Hughes handed her some index cards on which her lines were typed in red ink. Unfortunately, the lights in the theater were also red, so when she looked at the cards they appeared to be blank.[169]

• Interesting mishaps occur on stage. While dancing the lead in *Giselle*, ballerina Alicia Markova attempted to pluck a flower from the stage. However, the flower would not be plucked. Looking at the stage flowers, Ms. Markova discovered that they had all been nailed down by the stagehands. By giving the flower a mighty wrench, she was able to pluck it and continue with her dance.[170]

• George M. Cohan was famous as an actor, playwright, and producer. Once, he saw an advertisement asking for an actor who looked like George M. Cohan and who was able to impersonate George M. Cohan. For fun, Mr. Cohan decided to answer the ad, but the agent who had put the ad in the newspaper looked him over and said, "No use even considering you—you're not the type."[171]

• In 1732, the Italian castrato Senesino (original name: Francesco Bernardi) had just sung in *Giulio Cesare in Egitto* the line "Caesar does not know what fear is" when a piece of scenery fell near him. Senesino promptly threw himself to the floor and cried.[172]

Money

• Jazz musician Osie Johnson had a resonant voice, which he used one day when the Billy Williams Quartet was recording a song. They tried seven or eight times, but something went wrong each time. Finally, they got through the song, but as the last note was still sounding, Mr. Johnson burst out with a mighty "OH, YEAH!" Everyone was shocked because when someone is recording a song, guests aren't supposed to make a sound until the red recording light goes off, but Mr. Williams said, "That's great! Leave it in!" They listened to the recording of the song, and everyone realized that Mr. Williams was right—Mr. Johnson's "OH, YEAH!" was the perfect way to end the song. In fact, Mr. Williams paid Mr. Johnson for the "OH, YEAH!"[173]

• Richard Brinsley Sheridan, author of *The School for Scandal*, was chronically in debt. In 1816, while on his deathbed, he was arrested for debt and was nearly hauled off to jail. Fortunately, his physician stopped the arrest by telling the arresting officers that the move would kill Sheridan and that he would hold the arresting officers responsible for Sheridan's death. When Mr. Sheridan died, a bailiff disguised himself as a mourner and then arrested Sheridan's corpse because of a £500 debt. Only after a couple of Mr. Sheridan's friends wrote out checks did the bailiff allow Sheridan's corpse to be buried.[174]

• Boris Karloff's real name was William Henry Pratt. In 1887, he was born in London, but in the 1910s he went to Canada and became an actor. To get an acting job in repertory theater in British Columbia, he said that he was an experienced British stage actor. He got the job, and he went on stage, but when the curtain went up, his salary was $30 per week, and when the curtain went down, his salary was $15 a week—his performance showed quite clearly that he had never been on the stage before.[175]

• When Giulio Gatti-Casazza first became the director of the Metropolitan Opera in New York early in the 20th century, the women singers at the Met had a clause in their contracts saying that they would be paid even if they cancelled a scheduled performance because of indisposition. Not surprisingly, the singers were frequently indisposed. As soon as Gatti-Casazza became director, he cancelled that clause of their contracts. Not surprising, the cases of indisposition immediately declined in number.[176]

• After the premiere of his Ninth Symphony, Ludwig van Beethoven dedicated it to the King of Prussia, Friedrich Wilhelm II, sending the King a copy of the score. The King sent Beethoven a note of thanks, explaining that he was also sending him a diamond ring to show his appreciation. Because Beethoven needed money, he took the ring to a jeweler to have it appraised—and discovered that the "diamond" was a virtually worthless imitation.[177]

• Actor David Garrick had a reputation for being tight with his money. One day, he discovered that he had dropped a guinea while out for a walk, so he and Samuel Foote looked for it. While looking, Mr. Foote murmured, "Where can it have gone?" Mr., Garrick replied irritably, "To the devil, I think!" Remembering Mr. Garrick's tightness, Mr. Foote joked, "Ah, Davy, you alone could make a guinea go further than anybody else."[178]

• Francis X. Bushman made millions of dollars in the silent-film era—before income tax was instituted. Theatrical guru Danny Newman got to know him when Mr. Bushman was doing theater and was not making nearly as much money as in his days of silent-film stardom, Mr. Newman asked him, "Frank, what happened to all those millions you earned?" Mr. Bushman grinned happily and replied, "I *spent* them!"[179]

• Alexandra Danilova and George Balanchine once lived together in Monte Carlo, but when they were ready to leave, they didn't have enough money to pay their hotel bill. Mr. Balanchine said, "Let's go to the casino." They went there, and he quickly won 600 francs. He wanted to continue to gamble, so Ms. Danilova gave him 100 francs and took the rest to pay their bill before he lost all the money.[180]

• One way to see how successful a singer is, is to judge the singer's vocal quality. Another way is to look in the financial books and count the money paid by people to hear the singer. When Barbaja, a 19th-century impresario, was asked his opinion of one of his singers, he replied, "I have not yet consulted my books. I must see what the receipts were, and I will answer your question tomorrow."[181]

• Miss Anne Nichols spent five days writing the play *Abie's Irish Rose*, which critics of the 1920s such as Robert Benchley hated, but which audiences of the 1920s loved. At one point in its long run, she had made $10 million in profits from writing the play—$2 million for each day she had spent writing it.[182]

• Conductor Herbert von Karajan of the Berlin Philharmonic had a sense of humor. During a recording session, Plácido Domingo's European agent convinced him to record an extra take of a section of the opera *Turandot* by offering him a bribe of two German marks—worth at the time about 40 cents.[183]

Music

• Here are a few anecdotes about music and dance: 1) In 1597, Thomas Morley published a book titled *A Plaine and Easie Introduction to Practicall Musicke* that stressed that the ability to sing is a necessary part of every well-born person's education. As evidence, Mr. Morley relates this story about himself: "Supper being ended, and the Musicke bookes, according to the custome being brought to the table, the mistresse of the house presented mee with a part, earnestly requesting mee to sing. But when, after many excuses, I protested unfainedly that I could not: everie one began to wonder. Yea, some whispered to others, demanding how I was brought up." 2) In 1877 in Moscow Pyotr Ilich Tchaikovsky's *Swan Lake* was first performed, but only around two-thirds of his music was used because the dancers felt that it was just too difficult to dance to. 3) Johann Sebastian Bach composed the famous *B-Minor Mass*. Its name comes from its opening, which is in B minor, although most of the Mass is in D major. 4) Everyone is familiar with the tune known as "Here Comes the Bride." However, not everyone knows that it comes from Act III of Richard Wagner's *Lohengrin*.[184]

• Here are some music anecdotes: 1) Ezio Pinza worked as a six-day cyclist before becoming famous as a singer of grand opera. Once he was asked what six-day cyclists did after retiring from their sport. He replied, "They can open bicycle shops, as many do—or go into grand opera, as I did." 2) Enrico Caruso often made jokes. Once when a soprano was belting out an aria, he looked into her wide-open mouth and asked, "How would you like a nice, juicy steak?" 3) Jenny Lind, the Swedish Nightingale, was amazingly generous when giving to charity.

In 1850, while being managed by P. T. Barnum, she made $130,000 during a singing tour in the United States. She gave $100,000 of the money to charities in Sweden.[185]

• Some lawyers and judges in England tend not to think highly of music, or of composers, conductors, and musicians. Once, conductor Thomas Beecham was at a party where it was mentioned that a young man was studying to be a musician. A judge at the party asked, "Why doesn't he go into some honest trade?" At a court hearing, one of Beecham's lawyers mentioned the "musical profession," and a judge asked, "What's that? You don't call music a profession, do you?" On yet another occasion in court, after learning that Beecham had spent a great deal of money on music, the judge asked, "What is the good of that?"[186]

Names

• Alicia Markova, born Alicia Marks, was an English ballerina who was given her name by Russian ballet producer Sergei Diaghilev because at that time, ballet was not prominent in England although it was prominent in Russia. The name—and her reluctance to make speeches—fooled some journalists, who reported that Ms. Markova could not speak English! By the way, famous people get food and drink named after them. In Johannesburg, South Africa, there was once a Markova-Dolin cocktail, named after the ballet pair Alicia Markova and Anton Dolin, but Ms. Markova confessed that she lacked the courage to drink one.[187]

• Gaëtan Vestris (1728-1808) was the father of Auguste Vestris (1760-1842). Both were dancers, and as Gaëtan listened to and enjoyed the praise that was showered on Auguste's dancing, he remarked that of course Auguste had something that he had never had—the advantage of himself as his father. As a dance teacher later in his life, Auguste was called by his students "Grandpapa Zephyr."[188]

• Theatrical maven George Abbott was a man of dignity, and everyone called him Mr. Abbott. He once requested of a young man,

"Please call me George." The young man replied, "I certainly will, Mr. Abbott."[189]

Nudity

• The Broadway hippie musical *Hair* included a nude scene in which members of the cast stood facing the audience. The genesis of the nude scene came from a Be-in that 10,000 hippies attended in Central Park. Two male hippies took off their clothes, mounted police officers started coming to arrest them, and all the hippies faced the police officers and chanted, "We love cops. We love cops." This gave the naked hippies time to put their clothing back on and blend in with the crowd, so no one was arrested. *Hair* co-writer James Rado says, "It was the perfect hippie happening, and we felt it had to be in the play."[190]

• David Storey's play *The Changing Room* was set in a room where soccer players met before, during, and after a game. At one point in the play, the actors were made nervous because of a mysterious series of clicks coming from the audience—clicks they thought at first were made by the cocking (carefully chosen word, that) of pistols. Eventually, they figured out what was happening. The clicks occurred when the actors took off their shorts before going into the showers, and the clicks were made by binoculars tapping on eyeglasses as members of the audience took a close look.[191]

• Heather MacRae, the daughter of Gordon and Sheila MacRae, got her start in the musical *Hair*, where she was told that she could earn extra money if she took her clothing off for a scene. However, her mother told Heather that she would give her extra money if Heather kept her clothing on for that scene. Fortunately, Heather moved on to performing in other plays that did not give her the option of taking off her clothing. For these plays, she had to remain clad.[192]

Origins

• Good things — and good stories — can come from small beginnings: 1) The Fastbacks were a punk band from Seattle, Washington, that was formed by Kurt Bloch, Lulu Gargiulo, and Kim

Warnick. Ms. Gargiulo remembers, "The point when I decided, 'Okay, I'm going to play in a band — I'm going to do this myself' is [when] I went to this concert, and it was just the worst band. They weren't a punk band; they were just kind of a rock band. They were so bad that I told Kurt, 'These guys are so bad that I'm going to go start a band just to prove that I'm better than these guys.' So I got Kim and Kurt to sign up, you know ...." So how'd it go? Ms. Gargiulo remembers, "We just started playing, and it was really bad. ... I'll tell you, it was just horrible." They got better. Ms. Warnick remembers some of the memorable concerts the Fastbacks did: "Opening for Joan Jett at Wrex; opening for the Ramones in 1983 or '84 at the Eagles auditorium; the shows in Japan with Seaweed and the Supersuckers in 1993; and all the Pearl Jam concerts in 1996, where we went as far as Istanbul and we finally realized our ultimate rock and rock fantasy. Seeing the enormo-domes of the world *and* playing them was killer." 2) Kim Deal became a member of the Pixies through an audition for a bassist. How did she win the audition? She was the only person to show up. 3) Penelope Houston became lead singer of the San Francisco band Avengers almost by accident. She remembers, "I had some friends at the Art Institute that were starting a band. One day I was in their warehouse, and they had a PA set up. I had never sung through a microphone before. They were gone for the day, so I had six or seven hours to sing along with records. I found it so powerful to have this PA. They came back, and I said, "Well, you've got your lead singer right here!" They wrote seven songs in a week, and she worried, "How are we gonna remember all these songs?" The first time they played together, some incorrect playlists caused a problem. In the middle of some major discord stood Ms. Houston, who was thinking, "I can't remember how this song goes." After about 90 seconds, everyone stopped playing and began to ask, "What are you playing?" Finally, they figured out that the guitar player was playing one song while the bass player and the drummer were playing another song. 4) The Germs also got a little ahead of themselves. They started wearing band T-shirts and plastered Los Angeles, California, with band posters before writing any songs. 5) Did you know that the Adverts' first single, released on Stiff Records in 1977, was titled "One Chord Wonders"? 6) One more story: Poly Styrene of X-Ray Spex said that she would shave her head if she ever became a sex symbol. She did become a sex symbol — and she shaved her head. 7) I lied — here's another story: Susie Quatro also rejected becoming a sex symbol. She was a 1974 centerfold for *Penthouse* — despite being fully dressed.[193]

Parties

• Jerry Herman wrote the scores for many great Broadway musicals, including *Mame* and *Hello, Dolly!* and *Mack & Mabel*, among others. His mother seems to have been much like Mame. One day, when Jerry was a schoolboy, he came home from school and saw that his mother was hosting a party. He asked her what they were celebrating. Was it someone's birthday, was it an anniversary, was it an obscure holiday? His mother enthusiastically told him, "No, Jerry—it's TODAY!"[194]

• At one time, few artists were invited to the White House. However, when the Kennedys threw a party to honor French Minister of Culture Andre Malraux, lots of American artists were invited to attend. Writer Thornton Wilder was so pleased that at the party he told his friends, "Darlings, they let us in! At last they let us in!"[195]

Playwrights

• Here are some Brendan Behan anecdotes: 1) On a very cold day, Irish playwright Brendan Behan looked across the street and saw a woman who wrote about nature. Taking advantage of the situation, he yelled at her, "Hey, missus, how's the blue tits?" (Blue tits are, among other things, a species of bird.) 2) Brendan Behan once helped to bust an Irish Republican Army member out of prison—his duty was to make sure a Park Ranger did not make an outcry. Afterward, Mr. Behan praised the cooperation of the Park Ranger, saying the only thing he had to do to get his cooperation was "to hold a .45 revolver to his head all the time. Cocked." 3) Bill, the son of John B. Keane, once told Brendan Behan, "Don't drink anymore." Mr. Behan replied, "Whatever you say, Bill, but I'll have just one more to wash the last one down."[196]

• While watching a rehearsal of *Captain Brassbound's Conversion*, featuring actress Ellen Terry, a friend asked George Bernard Shaw if Ms. Terry was saying the lines as he had written them. Mr. Shaw replied, "No—but she is saying them as I ought to have written them."[197]

Politics

• Here are some Irish playwright Brendan Behan anecdotes: 1) Mr. Behan once promised to paint the apartment of poet Patrick Kavanagh absolutely free of charge while Mr. Kavanagh was away from home. He lived up to his promise—but he painted the apartment all black. 2) A prisoner on death row once asked Brendan Behan whether hanging was painful. Mr. Behan said that he thought it wasn't painful; however, he added, "I've never been through it myself, nor have I spoken to anyone who has." 3) The mother of Irish playwright Brendan Behan once said she wanted to see Paris before she died. Her husband said, "There's not much chance of you seeing it afterwards."[198]

• In Parliament was a Member who constantly interrupted speakers with cries of "Hear! Hear!" Detesting such a pompous fool, playwright/politician Richard Brinsley Sheridan set a trap for him. During a speech, he asked rhetorically, "Where oh where shall we find a more foolish knave or a more knavish fool than this?" As usual, the Member interrupted with his cry of "Hear! Hear!"[199]

Chapter 5: From Practical Jokes to Work

Practical Jokes

• Keith Moon, drummer of The Who, enjoyed pranking people. He used to have a friend go into a clothing store and request a pair of trousers made of very strong material. Mr. Moon would then enter the store and offer to help the friend test the strength of the material. He and the friend would each grab a trouser leg and rip the pair of trousers in half, and the friend would complain to the salesclerk about the shoddy material of the trousers. Then came the masterstroke: A one-legged actor would enter the store and say that he wanted to buy half a pair of trousers.[200]

• Frequently, telephones are used in the theater to play practical jokes on the actors on stage. (The actress on stage may be making a serious dramatic speech, while the practical joker on the other end of the telephone line is telling her funny stories.) Once, Eve Arden was on stage when the telephone began ringing when it wasn't supposed to. She looked at her co-star, who was also on stage, saw the hint of a smile, and realized that a practical joke was planned for her. So Ms. Arden answered the telephone, then handed it to her co-star, saying "It's for you."[201]

• Peter Ustinov once tried to make a date for lunch with Lord Rank, a film executive. Mr. Ustinov named date after date, but Lord Rank kept looking in his appointment book and finding that he was already scheduled to do something else that day. Finally, Lord Rank named a day four weeks in the future. Mr. Ustinov replied immediately, "So sorry—that's the one date I can't make."[202]

• Actor John Liston once played a practical joke on Mrs. Stephen Kemble while she was acting the role of Ophelia in *Hamlet*. Actresses in the role used to carry a basket filled with flowers on stage, but

Mr. Liston gave Mrs. Kemble a basket filled with onions, carrots, and turnips.[203]

Prejudice

• Eleanor Powell and the black dancer Bill Robinson, aka Mr. Bojangles, once performed at a private party put on by rich people. When the performance was over, Ms. Powell told the butler that she would like a glass of water—but only if Mr. Bojangles were also offered a glass of water. The butler brought them two glasses of water. Mr. Bojangles broke his glass after drinking the water, and he offered to pay for the glass. He told Ms. Powell later that he had broken the glass because he knew that no one would use the glass after he had used it. [204]

• After Lorraine Hansberry's play, *A Raisin in the Sun*, won several awards, including being named Best Play of the Season by the New York Critics Circle, making her the first African American and the youngest person ever to win the award, some people criticized her by saying that she had won the award only because she was an African American. She responded, "If I received the award because I am a Negro, then that's the first award given to a Negro!"[205]

Problem-Solving

• The late 18th- and early 19th-century actress Dora Jordan once appeared as Roxalana in *The Sultan* before an audience which contained enemies of hers who loudly criticized her. She stopped acting, walked to the footlights, and spoke directly to the audience: "Ladies and gentlemen, I should consider myself utterly unworthy of your favor if the slightest mark of public disapproval did not sensibly affect me. Ever since I have had the honor to strive here to please you, it has been my constant endeavor to merit your approbation. I assure you upon my honor that I have never absented myself one moment from my duties but from real indisposition. Ladies and gentlemen, I place myself under your protection." This speech won over the audience to her side, and her enemies quickly left the theater.[206]

• Franz Liszt was a famous pianist and of course people often asked him to play, which often he was unwilling to do. Count Hatzfeldt, the German ambassador to England, decided to trick Liszt into playing. He invited Liszt to a reception, and he had his piano pushed into a corner and covered with books and papers—that way, Liszt would not think that he had been invited to play the piano. At the reception, Count Hatzfeldt talked about music, mentioned a tune he had heard, and then went over to the piano, moved the books and papers off it and played a few notes. Liszt said, "No, it is not quite that," and then he sat at the piano and played the tune. Having played that tune, he then played a few other selections—to a very appreciative audience.[207]

• Audiences tend to think of acting as a glamorous job, but often actors have their problems on the stage. Agnes Booth played Belinda Treherne in W.S. Gilbert's satirical play *Engaged* when it was presented at Madison Square Garden over a century ago, but her role necessitated the eating of a great many tarts, and at length she rebelled. Fortunately, a pastry cook devised a satisfactory substitute made mostly of air (no filling). In fact, Ms. Booth did not need to eat anything, as the counterfeit tart was collapsible, and with some dexterity she was able to pretend to consume the "tarts." Theater critic John Rankin Towse wrote, "Thus the comedy went on, and the tarts were satisfactorily consumed without being eaten."[208]

• Henry Ford was an anti-Semite who backed the anti-Semitic publication the *Dearborn Independent*. This publication was about to start a series of articles railing against Jewish influence in Hollywood. Dore Schary, a film producer and the author of the play *Sunrise at Campobello*, showed Mr. Ford a short public-service documentary about automobile safety. The documentary showed a lot of automobile crashes—all of the crashing automobiles were Fords. The *Dearborn Independent* shelved its series of articles railing against Jewish influence in Hollywood, and Mr. Schary shelved his short public-service documentary about automobile safety.[209]

• Russian bass Fyodor Chaliapin enjoyed nights out on the town, and often the next morning his throat was totally unsuited for singing. But by the time the curtain rose that evening, he was able to hit high and middle notes, but not the soft notes. Still, he was known for his *pianissimo* notes, even after a night of drinking. How did he do it? He opened his mouth, concentrated, and raised his hand as if guiding very low notes toward the heavens. Through his considerable acting ability, he was able to convince the audience that they were hearing very soft notes although he was making absolutely no sound.[210]

• James Burbage constructed a playhouse known as the Theatre on rented land, but when his lease was almost over, he ran into problems with the landlord. Not wanting his lease to run out and not wanting to lose possession of the Theatre, Mr. Burbage solved the problem during the night of 28 December 1598. Under cover of darkness, he and his men tore down the Theatre and transported its materials to another site. The materials were used in the construction of the Globe, where William Shakespeare presented many of his plays.[211]

• Faustina Bordoni and Francesca Cuzzoni were rivals as opera singers, and both sang for George Frederic Handel. Eventually, it became clear that the two singers could not work together because of their rivalry, so one of them had to go. Because Ms. Bordoni was easier to get along with than Ms. Cuzzoni, she got to keep her job. To get rid of Ms. Cuzzoni was easy—Ms. Bordoni was offered a salary one guinea higher than Ms. Cuzzoni's salary, and Ms. Cuzzoni immediately quit. [212]

• Giuseppe Verdi was bothered by the censors, who forced him to make many changes to his *Rigoletto*. Because Verdi didn't want the censors to change the aria "*La Donna è Mobile*," he didn't show it to the censors; instead, he kept it hidden and gave it to the tenor the day before the opening. Verdi had so much trouble with the censors that eventually he suggested that the opera should be advertised as *Rigoletto: Poetry and Music by the Censors*.[213]

• Anthony Hopkins and Judi Dench starred in George Bernard Shaw's *Caesar and Cleopatra* in 1987. One night the audience kept coughing, and Ms. Dench complained, "I can't hear myself." Therefore, Mr. Hopkins suggested, "Why don't we just do the whole thing very fast, just rattle through it? That's shut them up." It worked. They spoke so quickly that the audience was afraid to cough, for fear of missing something.[214]

• During a tour in Australia, comic singer Anna Russell performed in a town hall that was being renovated and offered little protection from the elements (only a tarpaulin was between Ms. Russell and the cold). After turning purple in her evening gown, she told the audience that since they had seen the gown, she was going to dress more warmly, and she performed the rest of the concert wearing a football jersey over her evening gown.[215]

• Constance Benson (1860-1946) was an actress who toured with a company that frequently hired local actors as needed to swell its ranks. Unfortunately, these actors, including child actors, were often not very clean. When Ms. Benson played Titania in Shakespeare's *Midsummer's Night's Dream*, she used to unobtrusively sprinkle flea powder around the stage before her character fell asleep.[216]

• At one time, cellists held the cello between their knees while they played it instead of resting it on the floor. François Servais (1807-1866) was responsible for the peg on the bottom of the cello that enables it to be set on the floor as it is played. The innovation came about because of necessity—Mr. Servais' stomach became so fat that he no longer was able to hold the cello between his knees.[217]

• Vicious rumors frequently circulated about the famous early Shakespearean actress Dora Jordan. While in Bath, she stopped at the Pump Room, where she overheard a group of gossips saying vile things about her. She remained quiet, and soon a man came into the Pump Room and asked for Mrs. Jordan. She stood up, smiled sweetly at the astonished gossips, and left.[218]

• What can you do when a drunken man tries to pick a fight with you by yelling, "What are you lookin' at?" Illusionist Derren Brown had an interesting answer to this question when this situation happened to him. He replied, "The wall outside my house isn't 4ft high." He wanted to confuse the drunken man, but instead the drunken man started crying.[219]

• Soprano Frances Alda was bothered by a wolf whose reputation had preceded him. She asked him, "Do you know what I've heard about you? That you fall in love with every opera singer. I've heard that you were in love with Frances Saville." The wolf replied, "I was." Ms. Alda then said, "She is my aunt." Hearing that, the wolf left her alone.[220]

• Uninhibited actress Tallulah Bankhead once ran into a problem at the Café de Paris because she was wearing trousers, and at the time women visiting cabarets were not supposed to wear trousers. She easily and quickly solved the problem. She took off the trousers and walked into the Café de Paris in her underwear.[221]

• When theatrical producer Florenz "Flo" Ziegfeld fell in love with actress Billie Burke, he sent her basket after basket of flowers. She tried to telephone him to thank him, but his line was busy. When Flo heard about his line's being busy, he installed a special telephone just so she could call him whenever she wanted.[222]

Publicity

• Theatrical producer Florenz "Flo" Ziegfeld was a master of promotion. When he wanted to make Eugene Sandow, aka "the Strongest Man in the World," famous, he spent lots of money on advertisements and sold special tickets to society women in Chicago to allow them to go backstage after the show and to feel the Great Sandow's muscles. Once society leader Mrs. Potter Palmer had gone backstage and felt Mr. Sandow's muscles, everyone wanted to do the same thing, and Mr. Sandow's—and Flo's—success was assured. In addition, Flo arranged stunts to get publicity for Mr. Sandow. For example, while the two were traveling by train, Flo saw a huge iron wheel lying by the railroad track. He paid several men to put the heavy wheel in Mr. Sandow's compartment, and then he told reporters that Mr. Sandow was keeping it as a souvenir of his journey.[223]

• Henry Russell, the founder of the Boston Opera Company, understood publicity and how to get it. When the Boston Opera Company first performed Debussy's *Pelléas et Mélisande*, he told the press that Belgian playwright Maurice Maeterlinck would attend the performance. In addition, he told the press that he would award $1,000 to the author of the first interview with Mr. Maeterlinck, who was notorious for never giving interviews. Members of the press were very interested in the award and carefully scrutinized every incoming ship to see if Mr. Maeterlinck was on board; in addition, the press gave vast publicity to the Boston Opera Company. (What Mr. Russell didn't tell the press was that Mr. Maeterlinck had absolutely no intention of coming to USAmerica and attending the performance.)[224]

• While touring in California, Sarah Bernhardt used as her publicity man Sam Davis, who worked for both the Carlson *Appeal* and the San Francisco *Examiner*, as well as for the Associated Press. Mr. Davis was a very competent publicity man, and one day Ms. Bernhardt gave him a series of three kisses, saying, "The right cheek for the Carlson *Appeal*, the left for the San Francisco *Examiner*, and the mouth for you." Mr. Davis then said, "Madame, may I remind you that I also represent the Associated Press, which serves 380 newspapers west of Kansas."[225]

• Press agents used to do wild things to get their clients' names in the newspapers. Operatic tenor Leo Slezak once read in a newspaper that he always sang in public in bare feet. One audience that had read the same newspaper article became angry because he sang before them while wearing patent leather shoes. While in Chicago, opera stars Leo Slezak and Emmy Destinn were invited to a circus to name a baby camel as a publicity stunt. Ms. Destinn named the baby camel "Leo," and Mr. Slezak promised to name the next-born rhinoceros "Emmy." [226]

• Actor Val Vousden once asked the ringmaster of a circus in Ireland to give some publicity to his play, a historical drama titled *Robert Emmett*, in which he starred as the title character. The ringmaster obliged by saying, "If you want to see how Ireland has suffered and is suffering still, go and see Val Vousden play Robert Emmett!"[227]

Revenge

• Robert Loraine was a forceful actor. When he was starring as Othello, the actress playing Desdemona, Elissa Landi, protested at the violence he displayed in the final scene in which he strangled her, but Mr. Loraine covered her face with a pillow, saying, "You mind your own business, my dear lady, and I'll mind mine." He was also very egotistical. He ordered the company off the stage at one point so that he could take a curtain call alone, but the actor playing Iago, Ion Swinley, who was not egotistical but who was angry at Mr. Loraine's arrogance, refused to leave the stage, which forced Mr. Loraine to pretend in front of the audience that he enjoyed sharing the curtain call. Mr. Loraine did receive his comeuppance later, during a revival of *Cyrano*. He mistreated the stagehands, who got revenge by deliberately not securing the stage tree Cyrano sits under in the last act, forcing Mr. Loraine to act before the audience as he used his back to hold up the sagging tree.[228]

• In the days of vaudeville, theater owners were little tyrants who could take advantage of the acts that made them money. For example, one trick they pulled was to post a little "No Smoking" sign in a hard-to-see place and then fine performers for smoking although they had not seen the sign. This happened to Groucho Marx of the Marx Brothers once. It made him angry, and it made his brothers angry, and they told the theater owner that they were not going to perform unless the theater owner agreed not to fine Groucho. The audience grew restless and started stamping their feet and yelling, and the theater owner gave in and agreed not to fine Groucho. But the theater owner got his revenge; when he paid the Marx Brothers their wages, he paid them in big bags of pennies.[229]

• As a young soldier during World War II, Spike Milligan disliked the singing of Lance Bombardier Dodds, who enjoyed singing arias by Puccini a quarter-note flat after lights were out. Mr. Milligan decided to take action, so he filled a bucket with water, and as Lance Bombardier Dodds was singing, he opened the door. Lance Bombardier Dodds heard the door open, so he called, "Who is it?" Mr. Milligan replied, "Puccini," and threw the water on him.[230]

Theater

• Many people in the performing arts are superstitious: 1) In the theater, whistling is regarded as bringing bad luck. This superstition goes back to the days when curtains were drawn up and lowered by hand, and stagehands received their orders from the stage manager, who whistled when it was time to raise or lower the curtain. Anyone whistling in a theater back then could bring disaster to a stage production. 2) At one time real food was considered to be unlucky on stage, and so actors ate some very unappetizing "food" items. For example, "bacon" consisted of strips of bread coated with gravy, "tomatoes" consisted of circles of bread colored red, and "fried eggs" consisted of circles of bread with a little mustard in the middle. 3) Actress Tallulah Bankhead was very superstitious. For example, visitors to her dressing room had to use their right foot to step into it—visitors who used their left foot were told to go outside and then reenter it with their right foot first. In addition, she believed that champagne was lucky, and so she used to drink it before and during performances.[231]

• Here are some theater anecdotes: 1) Playwright Eugene O'Neill is the son of actor James O'Neill. Early in his career, Eugene O'Neill's plays were rejected by George C. Tyler, who didn't even bother to read them because, he explained, "Plays by actors' sons are never any good."

2) George M. Cohan, reputed to be the first actor to ever own a car, had an interesting way of writing plays. He used to write an act, rehearse it, and then write the next act, rehearse it, etc. 3) Florenz Ziegfeld was profligate with money. Sometimes he would have an idea for publicity and send a 1000-word telegram to his press agent, only to announce at the end of the telegram that the idea was bad and to forget about it. [232]

• Pearl Bailey sometimes stepped out of character as an actress. While starring in *Hello, Dolly*, she got a roar of applause as she walked down a stairway preparatory to singing her big number, so she asked the audience, "Want me to come down the stairs again?" They did, so she did.[233]

Tobacco

• Giovanni Mario (1810-1883) was an opera singer who greatly enjoyed smoking. Before he went on stage to perform, he always left a burning cigar where he would be able to enjoy it while he was out of sight of the audience. During a production of *Faust*, he walked through an onstage garden, going for a few moments behind some stage bushes. While he was behind the bushes, he enjoyed a few puffs of his cigar before walking again into the sight of the audience.[234]

• Famed Noh theater actor Roppeita Kita allowed Yousuf Karsh to take his photograph on the Noh theater stage, something that at one time he would not have permitted. However, following World War II, some American soldiers had given him cigarettes, so he felt that he should return the favor by allowing them to take his photograph. That had gotten him used to being photographed, and so he allowed Mr. Karsh to take that photograph.[235]

• Smoking can be dangerous to your health. Famed conductor Otto Klemperer once fell asleep while holding a lighted pipe—when he woke up, he was on fire.[236]

Travel

• Here are some Illaria Obidenna Ladré anecdotes: 1) As a ballerina, Illaria Obidenna Ladré danced all over the world. She learned from a mistake she made on her first trip to Australia. While on the ship, she and the troupe stopped working on pointe (that is, stopped practicing dancing on the tips of their toes). This made dancing on pointe for the first performance in Melbourne very painful. After that experience, she made practice on pointe a priority—but after ruining a pair of pointe shoes on deck, she learned how to practice in her tiny cabin. 2) William McDermott became a music conductor because he could stand working in high altitudes. During a trip with a ballet troupe to La Paz, Bolivia (located at an altitude of 14,000 feet), Mr. McDermott, who was a pianist, felt fine, but the regular conductor, Eugene Fuerst, fell victim to altitude sickness. Ballerina Illaria Obidenna Ladré suggested that Mr. McDermott conduct, and so he began his career as a conductor. 3) Early in the 20th century, ballet dancers didn't have a union to limit the length of rehearsals. Ballerina Illaria Obidenna Ladré once attended a rehearsal that lasted for 18 hours. (By the way, in the days before unions, ballet dancers weren't paid for rehearsals.)[237]

• Who drummer Keith Moon was hell on hotel rooms, and he and the other Who members were banned for life from the Holiday Inn hotel chain. Once, Mr. Moon carried bricks and mortar into his room, where he constructed a large dog kennel, which he cemented to the floor. He also did such things as driving a limousine into a Holiday Inn swimming pool, throwing several television sets out of various high windows, and nailing all the furniture to the ceiling.[238]

Vaudeville

• Here are some stories about Fred Allen, a comedian who started as a juggler in vaudeville: 1) Fred Allen wanted to attract the attention of New York booking agents while he was touring in vaudeville out West, so he kept mailing them gags. Once he mailed 100 bottles of brine, one each to 100 booking agents. Attached to each bottle was a label reading "Perspiration taken from the body of Freddy James [Mr. Allen's stage name at the time] after playing four shows a day at the Grand Theater." 2) While learning to juggle, Fred Allen juggled plates on a bed so that they wouldn't break if he dropped one. He also bought a top hat at a high price, because the seller told him that the hat had been specially balanced for juggling. He later learned that he could buy such "specially balanced" hats at the Salvation Army for 50 cents each. 3) Fred Allen's vaudeville act featured a spotlight shining on a placard that read, "Mr. Allen is quite deaf. If you care to LAUGH or APPLAUD, please do so LOUDLY."[239]

Wits

• The stage directions in the plays of lesbian performance artist Holly Hughes are often witty. For example, a stage direction in *The Well of Horniness* says, "Feel free to go too far; it's the only way to go in this play." And in *World Without End*, a stage direction refers to "an opportunity for acting, which I feel should be avoided at all costs." Later in *World Without End*, a stage direction refers to the music for a scene: "From offstage—left preferably—comes the sound of an accordion. I'd prefer a set of bagpipes, but an accordion is acceptable, considering the great shortage of accomplished lesbian bagpipe players. Not that I can tell the difference between well- and badly played bagpipes."[240]

• As everyone knows, Noël Coward was a witty man. When Lauren Bacall was about to star in *Applause*, he sent her this telegram: "DON'T BE NERVOUS, DARLING, BUT IT ALL DEPENDS ON YOU." She came through very well indeed, winning a Tony Award for her performance. Ms. Bacall's talent, besides acting, was stating what is on her mind. When she was 82 years old, a German journalist asked her if she ever thought about death. She replied, "You're a cheerful fellow, aren't you? Considering how close I am, don't you think that's a bit much?"[241]

• Here are two Richard Brinsley Sheridan stories: 1) When a rival playwright, Richard Cumberland, refused to laugh at Mr. Sheridan's comic play *The School for Scandal*, Mr. Sheridan said that he was hurt; after all, he had laughed heartily at Mr. Cumberland's recent tragedy. 2) Richard Brinsley Sheridan, the author of *The School for Scandal*, had many debts. Once, a creditor asked him to name a day on which a certain debt would be paid. Mr. Sheridan replied, "The Day of Judgment—but no, that is a busy day—make it the day after."[242]

• At Ferney, Voltaire had a church built. In it, he had a stage built for the performances of plays, saying, "If you meet any of the devout, tell them that I've built a church; if you meet pleasant people, tell them I've finished a theater."[243]

Work

• Acting leads to a dichotomy between reality and appearance. The 19th-century actor O. Smith remembers seeing the great John Kemble perform heroic roles of enormous valor and vigor near the end of his career. He also remembers Mr. Kemble being attended to by his servant during intermission. Because of Mr. Kemble's infirmity and asthma, the attendant was obliged to support him as he walked, but when Mr. Kemble was in front of an audience playing such characters as Cato, Cardinal Wolsey, and King John, no such support was necessary.[244]

• Sometimes kindness is ill repaid. Richard Ney once produced a musical titled *Portofino*. It ran into trouble during its pre-Broadway tour, and almost everyone felt that it would fail on Broadway. Mr. Ney called a meeting and asked the people in the show whether they should call it quits or continue on into New York and hope that the critics would like the show—a definite long shot. Everyone wanted the extra week of work, so they voted to go to New York. The critics absolutely detested *Portofino*, and Mr. Ney never produced another show.[245]

• Sir Rudolf Bing had a little trouble adjusting to life in America after leaving his native Europe. At a seedy hotel in New York, he followed the European custom of leaving his shoes outside his door (so they could be shined). The next morning, he discovered his shoes had been stolen. In 1949, Rudolf Bing, the general manager of the Metropolitan Opera, was told by a reporter for the *New York Herald Tribune*, "I am supposed to ask tactless questions." Mr. Bing replied, "Ah, yes, and I am supposed to give evasive answers."[246]

• Jerome K. Jerome (1859-1927) was a humorist who occasionally wrote for the theater. Once, a woman told him that she was sure he was capable of writing a play. Mr. Jerome replied that he had written nine plays. Of the nine, six were produced, and of the six, three were successful both in England and in America. Furthermore, one of his plays was in production right that moment and rapidly approaching its 200th performance. The woman raised her eyebrows and replied, "Dear me, you do surprise me."[247]

• Katja Biesanz once choreographed *The Marriage of Heaven and Earth*, a dance that needed a narrator. A dancer told her about a friend, a professional announcer, who could serve as narrator. Ms. Biesanz engaged the announcer for the performance, and he worked out marvelously—he had a wonderful voice and learned from direction well. But after the performance, Ms. Biesanz learned that the professional announcer was not an actor—he announced arrivals and departures at a bus terminal.[248]

• In the 1940s, being black could make it difficult to be in show business. African-American dancer Frances Nealy went to Hollywood, where she was told that movie producers wanted African-American actors to be darker than she. Later, in Atlantic City, she was lying in the sun, and she was told, "You better get out of that sun, or you won't be able to get a job! Because they really like the *lighter* girls."[249]

• World-famous conductor Thomas Beecham was occasionally annoyed by musicians' unions. At one rehearsal (not in England), an official of the union kept shouting out the minutes remaining until the rehearsal ended: "Fifteen minutes more," then "ten minutes more," then "only five minutes left." After this experience, Mr. Beecham threatened to quit if the interruptions ever happened again.[250]

• When Spike Milligan was being trained as a British soldier in World War II, the thing he had most trouble adjusting to was getting up at 6 in the morning. He used to envy the bugler who he says was able to stay in bed while blowing "Reveille" by pushing his door open with his foot. After waking up everybody in camp, the bugler then went back to sleep.[251]

• The nephew of internationally famous Austrian composer Anton Bruckner used to work as a head waiter at Niagara Falls. The nephew once told operatic tenor Leo Slezak that as he was growing up, his father used to tell him, "See that you don't turn out to be another miserable musician fellow like your Uncle Anton, or I'll wring your neck!"[252]

• Vaudeville was incredibly popular in the early 20th century. By the late teens, according to author Rusty E. Frank, "There were so many theaters on the vaudeville circuits that if an act had 14 good minutes, they could work six years without changing a word or playing the same theater twice."[253]

• Zero Mostel helped his friend Jack Gilford get a job acting in *A Funny Thing Happened on the Way to the Forum* by agreeing to read with him at his audition. Afterwards, at the end of each show of this huge success, Mr. Mostel would murmur to Mr. Gilford on stage, "Who got you this job?"[254]

• Early in her career, playwright Lorraine Hansberry was excited to receive a job as a production secretary. She hoped that the job would introduce her to the exciting world of theater, but she quit after discovering that the job mostly consisted of her serving coffee.[255]

• According to opera critic Barrymore Laurence Scherer, a good way to get information about an opera is to ask an usher—many of whom pride themselves on their knowledge of operas and many of whom take jobs as ushers simply to be near the opera.[256]

Appendix A: Bibliography

Alda, Frances. *Men, Women, and Tenors*. Boston, MA: Houghton Mifflin Company, 1937.

Allison, Amy. *Shakespeare's Globe*. San Diego, CA: Lucent Books, 2000.

Anecdotes of the Hour By Famous Men. New York: Hearst's International Library Company, 1914.

Atkinson, Margaret F. and May Hillman. *Dancers of the Ballet*. New York: Alfred A. Knopf, 1955.

Barber, David W. *If It Ain't Baroque ...: More Music History as It Ought to be Taught*. Toronto, Canada: Sound and Vision, 1992.

Barber, David W. *When the Fat Lady Sings: Opera History as It Ought to be Taught*. Toronto, Canada: Sound and Vision, 1990.

Beecham, Thomas. A *Mingled Chime*. New York: Da Capo Press, 1976.

Benson, Constance. *Mainly Players: Bensonian Memories*. London: Thornton Butterworth, Ltd., 1926.

Berry, Ralph, compiler and editor. *The Methuen Book of Shakespeare Anecdotes*. London: Methuen Drama, 1992.

Bing, Sir Rudolf. *5000 Nights at the Opera*. Garden City, NY: Doubleday and Company, Inc., 1972.

Block, Herbert. *Herblock: A Cartoonist's Life*. New York: Times Books, 1998.

Borge, Victor, and Robert Sherman. *My Favorite Intermissions*. Garden City, NY: Doubleday and Co., Inc., 1971.

Brandreth, Gyles. *Great Theatrical Disasters*. New York: St. Martin's Press, 1982.

Brook, Donald. *Singers of Today*. Freeport, New York: Books for Libraries Press, 1971.

Brown, Michèle and Ann O'Connor. *Hammer and Tongues: A Dictionary of Women's Wit and Humour*. London: J.M. Dent and Sons, Ltd., 1986.

Brubach, Holly. *Ten Dancers*. Photographs by Pierre Petitjean. New York: William Morrow and Company, Inc., 1982.

Bryan III, J. *Merry Gentlemen (and One Lady)*. New York: Atheneum, 1985.

Cantor, Eddie, and David Freedman. *Ziegfeld: The Great Glorifier*. New York: Alfred H. King, Inc., 1934.

Cavett, Dick. *Talk Show: Confrontations, Pointed Commentary, and Off-Screen Secrets*. New York: Henry Holt and Company, 2010.

Chapman, Graham. *Graham Crackers*. Compiled by Jim Yoakum. Franklin Lakes, NJ: Career Press, Inc., 1997.

Cooke, Alistair. *The Great and the Good*. New York: Arcade Publishing, 1999.

Crawford, John W. *Early Shakespearean Actresses*. New York: Peter Lang Publishing, Inc., 1984.

Danilova, Alexandra. *Choura: The Memoirs of Alexandra Danilova*. New York: Alfred A. Knopf, 1986.

de Mille, Agnes. *Portrait Gallery*. Boston, MA: Houghton Mifflin Company, 1990.

Dolin, Anton. *Alicia Markova: Her Life and Art*. New York: Hermitage House, 1953.

Domingo, Plácido. *My First Forty Years*. New York: Alfred A Knopf, 1983.

Donaldson, William. *Great Disasters of the Stage*. London: Arrow Books, Limited, 1984.

Drew, John. *My Years on the Stage*. New York: E.P. Dutton & Company, 1922.

Drennan, Robert E., editor. *The Algonquin Wits*. New York: The Citadel Press, 1968.

Duncan, Kenn. *Divas: The Fabulous Photography of Kenn Duncan*. New York: Universe Publishing, 2008. Text by Stephen M. Silverman.

Eichenbaum, Rose. *Masters of Movement: Portraits of America's Great Choreographers*. Washington, D.C.: Smithsonian Books, 2004.

Ewen, David, complier. *Listen to the Mocking Words*. New York: Arco Publishing Co., 1945.

Farrell, Suzanne. *Holding On to the Air*. New York: Summit Books, 1990.

Finck, Henry T. *Musical Laughs*. New York: Funk & Wagnalls Company, 1924.

Finck, Henry T. *My Adventures in the Golden Age of Music*. New York and London: Funk & Wagnalls Company, 1926.

Flagg, James Montgomery. *Roses and Buckshot*. New York: Van Rees Press, 1946.

Fonteyn, Margot. *Autobiography*. New York: Alfred A. Knopf, 1976.

Ford, Carin T. *Legends of American Dance and Choreography*. Berkeley Heights, NJ: Enslow Publications, Inc., 2000.

Frank, Rusty E. *Tap! The Greatest Tap Dance Stars and Their Stories, 1900-1955*. New York: William Morrow and Company, Inc., 1990.

Gielgud, John. *Distinguished Company*. London: Heinemann, 1972.

Gielgud, John, and John Miller. *Acting Shakespeare*. New York: Charles Scribner's Sons, 1991.

Goldsmith, Joan Oliver. *How Can We Keep from Singing: Music and the Passionate Life*. New York and London: W.W. Norton & Company, 2001.

Greskovic, Robert. *Ballet 101*. New York: Hyperion, 1998.

Hay, Peter. *Broadway Anecdotes*. New York: Oxford University Press, 1989.

Henry, Lewis C. *Humorous Anecdotes About Famous People*. Garden City, NY: Halcyon House, 1948.

Huggett, Richard. *Supernatural on Stage: Ghosts and Superstitions of the Theatre.* New York: Taplinger Publishing Company, 1975.

Humphrey, Laning, compiler. *The Humor of Music and Other Oddities in the Art.* Boston, MA: Crescendo Publishing Company, 1971.

Isenberg, Barbara. *State of the Arts: California Artists Talk About Their Work.* Chicago, IL: Ivan R. Dee, 2000.

Harris, Leon A. *The Fine Art of Political Wit.* New York: Dell Publishing Company, 1964.

Harris, Nick. *I Wish I'd Said That!* London: Octopus Books, Limited, 1984.

Haskins, Jim, and N.R. Mitgang. *Mr. Bojangles: The Story of Bill Robinson.* New York: William Morrow and Company, Inc., 1988.

Hecht, Ben. *Charlie: The Improbable Life and Times of Charles MacArthur.* New York: Harper & Brothers, Publishers, 1957.

Hewlett-Davies, Barry, editor and compiler. *A Night at the Opera.* New York: St. Martin's Press, 1980.

Hinton, Milt, David G. Berger, and Holly Maxson. *Playing the Changes: Milt Hinton's Life in Stories and Photographs.* Nashville, TN: Vanderbilt University Press, 2008.

Holloway, Stanley. *Wiv a Little Bit O' Luck.* As told to Dick Richards. New York: Stein and Day, Publishers, 1967.

Huggett, Richard. *Supernatural on Stage: Ghosts and Superstitions of the Theatre.* New York: Taplinger Publishing Company, 1975.

Hughes, Holly. *Clit Notes: A Sapphic Sampler.* New York: Grove Press, 1996.

Jerome, Jerome K. *On the Stage—and Off: The Brief Career of a Would-Be Actor.* Wolfeboro Falls, NH: Alan Sutton Publishing, Inc., 1991.

Karkar, Jack and Waltraud, compilers and editors. *... And They Danced On.* Wausau, WI: Aardvark Enterprises, 1989.

Karsh, Yousuf. *Faces of Our Time*. Toronto and Buffalo, NY: University of Toronto Press, 1971.

Kaufmann, Helen L. *Anecdotes of Music and Musicians*. New York: Grosset & Dunlap, Publishers, 1960.

Ladré, Illaria Obidenna. *Illaria Obidenna Ladré: Memoirs of a Child of Theatre Street*. With Nancy Whyte. Seattle, WA: The Author, 1988.

Laffey, Bruce. *Beatrice Lillie: The Funniest Woman in the World*. New York: Wynwood Press, 1989.

Legat, Nicolas. *Ballet Russe: Memoirs of Nicolas Legat*. Translated by Sir Paul Dukes. London: Methuen & Co., Ltd., 1939.

Linkletter, Art. *I Wish I'd Said That! My Favorite Ad-Libs of All Time*. Garden City, NY: Doubleday & Co., Inc., 1968.

Mapleson, Colonel J.H. *The Mapleson Memoirs: The Career of an Operatic Impresario, 1858-1888*. Edited by Harold Rosenthal. New York: Appleton-Century, 1966.

Makarova, Natalia. *A Dance Autobiography*. Edited by Gennady Smakov. New York: Alfred A Knopf, Inc., 1979.

Markova, Alicia. *Giselle and Me*. New York: The Vanguard Press, Inc., 1960.

Marinacci, Barbara. *Leading Ladies: A Gallery of Famous Actresses*. New York: Dodd, Mead and Company, 1961.

Markova, Alicia. *Markova Remembers*. Boston, MA: Little, Brown and Company, 1986.

Marx, Groucho. *Groucho Marx and Other Short Stories and Tall Tales*. Edited by Robert S. Bader. Boston, MA: Faber and Faber, 1996.

Marx, Samuel. *Broadway Portraits*. New York: Donald Flamm, Inc., 1929.

Massine, Léonide. *My Life in Ballet*. Edited by Phyllis Hartnoll and Robert Rubens. London: Macmillan and Co., Ltd., 1968.

Maurois, Andre. "An Appreciation." Introduction to Voltaire. *Candide*. New York: Bantam Books, 1959.

May, Robin, compiler. *The Wit of the Theatre*. London: Leslie Frewin, 1969.

McCann, Sean, compiler. *The Wit of Brendan Behan*. London: Leslie Frewin Publishers, Ltd., 1968.

McCann, Sean, compiler. *The Wit of the Irish*. Nashville, TN: Aurora Publishers, Ltd., 1970.

McMahon, Ed. *Here's Johnny! My Memories of Johnny Carson,* The Tonight Show, *and 46 Years of Friendship*. Nashville, TN: Rutledge Hill Press, 2005.

Miller, John. *Judi Dench: With a Crack in Her Voice*. New York: Welcome Rain Publishers, 2000.

Miller, John. *Ralph Richardson: The Authorized Biography*. London: Sidgwick and Jackson, 1995.

Milligan, Spike. *Adolf Hitler: My Part in His Downfall*. London: Michael Joseph, Limited, 1971.

Montague, Sarah. *Pas de Deux: Great Partnerships in Dance*. New York: Universe Books, 1981.

Morley, Robert. *Robert Morley's Book of Bricks*. New York: G.P. Putnam's Sons, 1979.

Mostel, Kate, and Madeline Gilford. *170 Years of Show Business*. With Jack Gilford and Zero Mostel. New York: Random House, 1978.

Nachman, Gerald. *Seriously Funny: The Rebel Comedians of the 1950s and 1960s*. New York: Pantheon Books, 2003.

Nardo, Don. *Greek and Roman Theater*. San Diego, CA: Lucent Books, 1995.

Neale, Wendy. *Ballet Life Behind the Scenes*. New York: Crown Publishers, Inc., 1982.

Newman, Danny. *Tales of a Theatrical Guru*. Urbana and Chicago, IL: University of Illinois Press, 2006.

Nicholson, Frank Ernest. *Favorite Jokes of Famous People*. New York: E.P. Dutton & Co., Inc., 1928.

Norkin, Sam. *Drawings, Stories: Theater, Opera, Ballet, Movies.* Portsmouth, NH: Heinemann, 1994.

Pearson, Hesketh. *Lives of the Wits.* New York: Harper & Row, Publishers, 1962.

Phillips, Julien. *Stars of the Ziegfeld Follies.* Minneapolis, MN: Lerner Publications Company, 1972.

Reflections: The Taper at Twenty. Los Angeles, California: Center Theatre Group/Mark Taper Forum, 1987.

Reiner, Carl. *My Anecdotal Life.* New York: St. Martin's Press, 2003.

Richards, Dick, compiler. *The Wit of Noël Coward.* London: Leslie Frewin, 1968.

Richards, Dick, compiler. *The Wit of Peter Ustinov.* London: Leslie Frewin Publishers, Limited, 1969.

Rigg, Diana, compiler. *No Turn Unstoned: The Worst Ever Theatrical Reviews.* Los Angeles, CA: Silman-James Press, 1982.

Rowland, Walter. *Among the Great Masters of the Drama.* Boston, MA: Dana Estes and Company, 1903.

Russell, Anna. *I'm Not Making This Up, You Know: The Autobiography of the Queen of Musical Parody.* New York: The Continuum Publishing Company, 1985.

Russell, Mark, editor. *Out of Character.* New York: Bantam Books, 1997.

Sankey, Jay. *Zen and the Art of Stand-Up Comedy.* New York: Routledge/Theatre Arts Books, 1998.

Scheader, Catherine. *Lorraine Hansberry: Playwright and Voice of Justice.* Springfield, NJ: Enslow Publications, Inc., 1998.

Scherer, Barrymore Laurence. *Bravo! A Guide to Opera for the Perplexed.* New York: Dutton, 1996.

Shawn, Ted. *One Thousand and One Night Stands.* With Gray Poole. New York: Da Capo Press, Inc., 1979.

Silverman, Stephen M. *Funny Ladies: The Women Who Make Us Laugh*. New York: Harry N. Abrams, Inc., 1999.

Slezak, Leo. *Song of Motley*. New York: Arno Press, 1977.

Slide, Anthony. *Eccentrics of Comedy*. Lanham, MD, and London: The Scarecrow Press, Inc., 1998.

Smith, H. Allen. *The Compleat Practical Joker*. Garden City, NY: Doubleday and Company, Inc., 1953.

Smith, H. Allen. *To Hell in a Handbasket*. Garden City, NY: Doubleday & Company, Inc., 1962.

Smith, O. *Recollections of O. Smith, Comedian*. New York: Theatre Library Association, 1979.

Stier, Theodore. *With Pavlova Around the World*. London: Hurst & Blackett, Ltd., 1927.

Suntree, Susan. *Rita Moreno*. New York: Chelsea House Publishers, 1993.

Tanner, Stephen. *Opera Antics and Anecdotes*. Toronto, Canada: Sound and Vision, 1999.

Terry, Walter. *Frontiers of Dance: The Life of Martha Graham*. New York: Thomas Y. Crowell Company, 1975.

Terry, Walter. *Ted Shawn: Father of American Dance*. New York: The Dial Press, 1976.

Towse, John Rankin. *Sixty Years of the Theater: An Old Critic's Memories*. New York and London: Funk & Wagnalls Company, 1916.

True, Everett. *Hey Ho Let's Go: The Story of the Ramones*. London: Omnibus Press, 2002.

Turk, Ruth. *Lillian Hellman: Rebel Playwright*. Minneapolis, MN: Lerner Publications Company. 1995.

Wagenknecht, Edward. *Merely Players*. Norman, OK: University of Oklahoma Press, 1966.

Wagner, Alan. *Prima Donnas and Other Wild Beasts*. Larchmont, NY: Argonaut Books, 1961.

Wallach, Eli. *The Good, the Bad, and Me: In My Anecdotage.* Orlando, FL: Harcourt, Inc., 2005.

Williams, Kenneth. *Acid Drops.* London: J. M. Dent & Sons, Ltd., 1980.

Woollcott, Alexander. *Enchanted Aisles.* New York: G.P. Putnam's Sons, 1924.

Woollcott, Alexander. *Shouts and Murmurs: Echoes of a Thousand and One Nights.* New York: The Century Co., 1922.

Woollcott, Barbara. *None But a Mule.* New York: The Viking Press, 1944.

Zolotow, Maurice. *No People Like Show People.* New York: Random House, 1951.

Appendix B: About the Author

It was a dark and stormy night. Suddenly a cry rang out, and on a hot summer night in 1954, Josephine, wife of Carl Bruce, gave birth to a boy — me. Unfortunately, this young married couple allowed Reuben Saturday, Josephine's brother, to name their first-born. Reuben, aka "The Joker," decided that Bruce was a nice name, so he decided to name me Bruce Bruce. I have gone by my middle name — David — ever since.

Being named Bruce David Bruce hasn't been all bad. Bank tellers remember me very quickly, so I don't often have to show an ID. It can be fun in charades, also. When I was a counselor as a teenager at Camp Echoing Hills in Warsaw, Ohio, a fellow counselor gave the signs for "sounds like" and "two words," then she pointed to a bruise on her leg twice. Bruise Bruise? Oh yeah, Bruce Bruce is the answer!

Uncle Reuben, by the way, gave me a haircut when I was in kindergarten. He cut my hair short and shaved a small bald spot on the back of my head. My mother wouldn't let me go to school until the bald spot grew out again.

Of all my brothers and sisters (six in all), I am the only transplant to Athens, Ohio. I was born in Newark, Ohio, and have lived all around Southeastern Ohio. However, I moved to Athens to go to Ohio University and have never left.

At Ohio U, I never could make up my mind whether to major in English or Philosophy, so I got a bachelor's degree with a double major in both areas, then I added a Master of Arts degree in English and a Master of Arts degree in Philosophy. Yes, I have my MAMA degree.

Currently, and for a long time to come (I eat fruits and veggies), I am spending my retirement writing books such as *Nadia Comaneci: Perfect 10*, *The Funniest People in Comedy*, *Homer's* Iliad: *A Retelling in Prose*, and *William Shakespeare's* Hamlet: *A Retelling in Prose*.

By the way, my sister Brenda Kennedy writes romances such as *A New Beginning* and *Shattered Dreams*.

Appendix C: Some Books by David Bruce

Anecdote Books

250 Anecdotes About Opera

250 Anecdotes About Religion

250 Anecdotes About Religion: Volume 2

The Coolest People in Art: 250 Anecdotes

The Coolest People in Books: 250 Anecdotes

The Coolest People in Comedy: 250 Anecdotes

Don't Fear the Reaper: 250 Anecdotes

The Funniest People in Art: 250 Anecdotes

The Funniest People in Books: 250 Anecdotes

The Funniest People in Books, Volume 2: 250 Anecdotes

The Funniest People in Books, Volume 3: 250 Anecdotes

The Funniest People in Comedy: 250 Anecdotes

The Funniest People in Dance: 250 Anecdotes

The Funniest People in Families: 250 Anecdotes

The Funniest People in Families, Volume 2: 250 Anecdotes

The Funniest People in Families, Volume 3: 250 Anecdotes

The Funniest People in Families, Volume 4: 250 Anecdotes

The Funniest People in Families, Volume 5: 250 Anecdotes

The Funniest People in Families, Volume 6: 250 Anecdotes

The Funniest People in Movies: 250 Anecdotes

The Funniest People in Music: 250 Anecdotes

The Funniest People in Music, Volume 2: 250 Anecdotes

The Funniest People in Music, Volume 3: 250 Anecdotes

The Funniest People in Neighborhoods: 250 Anecdotes

The Funniest People in Relationships: 250 Anecdotes

The Funniest People in Sports: 250 Anecdotes

The Funniest People in Sports, Volume 2: 250 Anecdotes

The Funniest People in Television and Radio: 250 Anecdotes
The Funniest People in Theater: 250 Anecdotes
The Funniest People Who Live Life: 250 Anecdotes
The Funniest People Who Live Life, Volume 2: 250 Anecdotes
The Kindest People Who Do Good Deeds, Volume 1: 250 Anecdotes
The Kindest People Who Do Good Deeds, Volume 2: 250 Anecdotes
Maximum Cool: 250 Anecdotes
The Most Interesting People in Movies: 250 Anecdotes
The Most Interesting People in Politics and History: 250 Anecdotes
The Most Interesting People in Politics and History, Volume 2: 250 Anecdotes
The Most Interesting People in Politics and History, Volume 3: 250 Anecdotes
The Most Interesting People in Religion: 250 Anecdotes
The Most Interesting People in Sports: 250 Anecdotes
The Most Interesting People Who Live Life: 250 Anecdotes
The Most Interesting People Who Live Life, Volume 2: 250 Anecdotes
Resist Psychic Death: 250 Anecdotes
Seize the Day: 250 Anecdotes and Stories

Children's Biography

Nadia Comaneci: Perfect Ten

Discussion Guides Series

Dante's Inferno: *A Discussion Guide*
Dante's Paradise: *A Discussion Guide*
Dante's Purgatory: *A Discussion Guide*
Forrest Carter's The Education of Little Tree: *A Discussion Guide*
Homer's Iliad: *A Discussion Guide*
Homer's Odyssey: *A Discussion Guide*
Jane Austen's Pride and Prejudice: *A Discussion Guide*
Jerry Spinelli's Maniac Magee: *A Discussion Guide*
Jerry Spinelli's Stargirl: *A Discussion Guide*
Jonathan Swift's "A Modest Proposal": A Discussion Guide

Lloyd Alexander's The Black Cauldron: *A Discussion Guide*

Lloyd Alexander's The Book of Three: *A Discussion Guide*

Lois Lowry's Number the Stars: *A Discussion Guide*

Mark Twain's Adventures of Huckleberry Finn: *A Discussion Guide*

Mark Twain's The Adventures of Tom Sawyer: *A Discussion Guide*

Mark Twain's A Connecticut Yankee in King Arthur's Court: *A Discussion Guide*

Mark Twain's The Prince and the Pauper: *A Discussion Guide*

Nancy Garden's Annie on My Mind: *A Discussion Guide*

Nicholas Sparks' A Walk to Remember: *A Discussion Guide*

Virgil's Aeneid: *A Discussion Guide*

Virgil's "The Fall of Troy": *A Discussion Guide*

Voltaire's Candide: *A Discussion Guide*

William Shakespeare's 1 Henry IV: *A Discussion Guide*

William Shakespeare's Macbeth: *A Discussion Guide*

William Shakespeare's A Midsummer Night's Dream: *A Discussion Guide*

William Shakespeare's Romeo and Juliet: *A Discussion Guide*

William Sleator's Oddballs: *A Discussion Guide*

(Oddballs is an excellent source for teaching how to write autobiographical essays/personal narratives.)

Retellings of a Classic Work of Literature

Arden of Faversham: *A Retelling*

Ben Jonson's The Alchemist: *A Retelling*

Ben Jonson's The Arraignment, or Poetaster: *A Retelling*

Ben Jonson's Bartholomew Fair: *A Retelling*

Ben Jonson's The Case is Altered: *A Retelling*

Ben Jonson's Catiline's Conspiracy: *A Retelling*

Ben Jonson's The Devil is an Ass: *A Retelling*

Ben Jonson's Epicene: *A Retelling*

Ben Jonson's Every Man in His Humor: *A Retelling*

Ben Jonson's Every Man Out of His Humor: *A Retelling*

Ben Jonson's The Fountain of Self-Love, or Cynthia's Revels: *A Retelling*

Ben Jonson's The Magnetic Lady, or Humors Reconciled: *A Retelling*

Ben Jonson's The New Inn, or The Light Heart: *A Retelling*

Ben Jonson's Sejanus' Fall: *A Retelling*

Ben Jonson's The Staple of News: *A Retelling*

Ben Jonson's A Tale of a Tub: *A Retelling*

Ben Jonson's Volpone, or the Fox: *A Retelling*

Christopher Marlowe's Complete Plays: Retellings

Christopher Marlowe's Dido, Queen of Carthage: *A Retelling*

Christopher Marlowe's Doctor Faustus: *Retellings of the 1604 A-Text and of the 1616 B-Text*

Christopher Marlowe's Edward II: *A Retelling*

Christopher Marlowe's The Massacre at Paris: *A Retelling*

Christopher Marlowe's The Rich Jew of Malta: *A Retelling*

Christopher Marlowe's Tamburlaine, Parts 1 and 2: *Retellings*

Dante's Divine Comedy: *A Retelling in Prose*

Dante's Inferno: *A Retelling in Prose*

Dante's Purgatory: *A Retelling in Prose*

Dante's Paradise: *A Retelling in Prose*

The Famous Victories of Henry V: *A Retelling*

From the Iliad *to the* Odyssey: *A Retelling in Prose of Quintus of Smyrna's* Posthomerica

George Chapman, Ben Jonson, and John Marston's Eastward Ho! *A Retelling*

George Peele's The Arraignment of Paris: *A Retelling*

George Peele's The Battle of Alcazar: *A Retelling*

George Peele's David and Bathsheba, and the Tragedy of Absalom: *A Retelling*

George Peele's Edward I: *A Retelling*

George Peele's The Old Wives' Tale: *A Retelling*

George-a-Greene: *A Retelling*

The History of King Leir: *A Retelling*

Homer's Iliad: *A Retelling in Prose*

Homer's Odyssey: *A Retelling in Prose*

J.W. Gent.'s The Valiant Scot: *A Retelling*

Jason and the Argonauts: A Retelling in Prose of Apollonius of Rhodes' Argonautica

John Ford: Eight Plays Translated into Modern English

John Ford's The Broken Heart: *A Retelling*

John Ford's The Fancies, Chaste and Noble: *A Retelling*

John Ford's The Lady's Trial: *A Retelling*

John Ford's The Lover's Melancholy: *A Retelling*

John Ford's Love's Sacrifice: *A Retelling*

John Ford's Perkin Warbeck: *A Retelling*

John Ford's The Queen: *A Retelling*

John Ford's 'Tis Pity She's a Whore: *A Retelling*

John Lyly's Campaspe: *A Retelling*

John Lyly's Endymion, The Man in the Moon: *A Retelling*

John Lyly's Galatea: *A Retelling*

John Lyly's Love's Metamorphosis: *A Retelling*

John Lyly's Midas: *A Retelling*

John Lyly's Mother Bombie: *A Retelling*

John Lyly's Sappho and Phao: *A Retelling*

John Lyly's The Woman in the Moon: *A Retelling*

John Webster's The White Devil: *A Retelling*

King Edward III: *A Retelling*

Mankind: *A Medieval Morality Play* (A Retelling)

Margaret Cavendish's The Unnatural Tragedy: *A Retelling*

The Merry Devil of Edmonton: *A Retelling*

The Summoning of Everyman: *A Medieval Morality Play* (A Retelling)

Robert Greene's Friar Bacon and Friar Bungay: *A Retelling*

The Taming of a Shrew: *A Retelling*

Tarlton's Jests: A Retelling

Thomas Middleton's A Chaste Maid in Cheapside: *A Retelling*

Thomas Middleton's Women Beware Women: *A Retelling*

Thomas Middleton and Thomas Dekker's The Roaring Girl: *A Retelling*

Thomas Middleton and William Rowley's The Changeling: *A Retelling*

The Trojan War and Its Aftermath: Four Ancient Epic Poems

Virgil's Aeneid: *A Retelling in Prose*

William Shakespeare's 5 Late Romances: Retellings in Prose

William Shakespeare's 10 Histories: Retellings in Prose

William Shakespeare's 11 Tragedies: Retellings in Prose

William Shakespeare's 12 Comedies: Retellings in Prose

William Shakespeare's 38 Plays: Retellings in Prose

William Shakespeare's 1 Henry IV, aka Henry IV, Part 1: *A Retelling in Prose*

William Shakespeare's 2 Henry IV, aka Henry IV, Part 2: *A Retelling in Prose*

William Shakespeare's 1 Henry VI, aka Henry VI, Part 1: *A Retelling in Prose*

William Shakespeare's 2 Henry VI, aka Henry VI, Part 2: *A Retelling in Prose*

William Shakespeare's 3 Henry VI, aka Henry VI, Part 3: *A Retelling in Prose*

William Shakespeare's All's Well that Ends Well: *A Retelling in Prose*

William Shakespeare's Antony and Cleopatra: *A Retelling in Prose*

William Shakespeare's As You Like It: *A Retelling in Prose*

William Shakespeare's The Comedy of Errors: *A Retelling in Prose*

William Shakespeare's Coriolanus: *A Retelling in Prose*

William Shakespeare's Cymbeline: *A Retelling in Prose*

William Shakespeare's Hamlet: *A Retelling in Prose*

William Shakespeare's Henry V: *A Retelling in Prose*

William Shakespeare's Henry VIII: *A Retelling in Prose*

William Shakespeare's Julius Caesar: *A Retelling in Prose*

William Shakespeare's King John: *A Retelling in Prose*

William Shakespeare's King Lear: *A Retelling in Prose*

William Shakespeare's Love's Labor's Lost: *A Retelling in Prose*

William Shakespeare's Macbeth: *A Retelling in Prose*

William Shakespeare's Measure for Measure: *A Retelling in Prose*

William Shakespeare's The Merchant of Venice: *A Retelling in Prose*

William Shakespeare's The Merry Wives of Windsor: *A Retelling in Prose*

William Shakespeare's A Midsummer Night's Dream: *A Retelling in Prose*

William Shakespeare's Much Ado About Nothing: *A Retelling in Prose*

William Shakespeare's Othello: *A Retelling in Prose*

William Shakespeare's Pericles, Prince of Tyre: *A Retelling in Prose*

William Shakespeare's Richard II: *A Retelling in Prose*

William Shakespeare's Richard III: *A Retelling in Prose*

William Shakespeare's Romeo and Juliet: *A Retelling in Prose*

William Shakespeare's The Taming of the Shrew: *A Retelling in Prose*

William Shakespeare's The Tempest: *A Retelling in Prose*

William Shakespeare's Timon of Athens: *A Retelling in Prose*

William Shakespeare's Titus Andronicus: *A Retelling in Prose*

William Shakespeare's Troilus and Cressida: *A Retelling in Prose*

William Shakespeare's Twelfth Night: *A Retelling in Prose*

William Shakespeare's The Two Gentlemen of Verona: *A Retelling in Prose*

William Shakespeare's The Two Noble Kinsmen: *A Retelling in Prose*

Appendix D: Some Books by Brenda Kennedy (My Sister)

The Forgotten Trilogy
    Book One: *Forgetting the Past*
    Book Two: *Living for Today*
    Book Three: *Seeking the Future*
    The Learning to Live Trilogy
    Book One: *Learning to Live*
    Book Two: *Learning to Trust*
    Book Three: *Learning to Love*
    The Starting Over Trilogy
    Book One: *A New Beginning*
    Book Two: *Saving Angel*
    Book Three: *Destined to Love*
    The Freedom Trilogy
    Book One: *Shattered Dreams*
    Book Two: *Broken Lives*
    Book Three: *Mending Hearts*
    The Fighting to Survive Trilogy
    Round One: *A Life Worth Fighting*
    Round Two: *Against the Odds*
    Round Three: *One Last Fight*
    The Rose Farm Trilogy
    Book One: *Forever Country*
    Book Two: *Country Life*
    Book Three: *Country Love*
    Books in the Seashell Island Stand-alone Series
    Book One: *Home on Seashell Island* (Free)
    Book Two: *Christmas on Seashell Island*
    Book Three: *Living on Seashell Island*
    Book Four: *Moving to Seashell Island*
    Book Five: *Returning to Seashell Island*
    Books in the Pineapple Grove Cozy Murder Mystery Stand-alone Series
    Book One: *Murder Behind the Coffeehouse*
    Book Two: *Murder in the Library*
    Books in the Montgomery Wine Stand-alone Series

Book One: *A Place to Call Home*

Book Two: *In Search of Happiness...* **coming soon**

Stand-alone books in the "Another Round of Laughter Series" written by Brenda and some of her siblings: Carla Evans, Martha Farmer, Rosa Jones, and David Bruce.

Cupcakes Are Not a Diet Food (Free)

Kids Are Not Always Angels

Aging Is Not for Sissies

---

[1] Source: Ben Primack, adapter and editor, *The Ben Hecht Show*, p. 22.

[2] Source: *Reflections: The Taper at Twenty*, p. 115.

[3] Source: Lucy Powell, "Atkins, the most 'astonishingly lucky person.'" *The Times.* 5 July 2008 <http://entertainment.timesonline.co.uk/tol/arts_and_entertainment/stage/theatre/article4255286.ece>.

[4] Source: Edward Wagenknecht, *Merely Players*, pp. 10-12, 23.

[5] Source: Xan Brooks, "Eva Green: 'Maybe I'll end up living in Norway, making cakes.'" *The Guardian.* 2 April 2010 <http://www.guardian.co.uk/film/2010/apr/02/eva-green-cracks-james-bond>.

[6] Source: Edward Wagenknecht, *Merely Players*, p. 175.

[7] Source: Ed Potton, "Brian Blessed, actor and adventurer, stars in *Peter and the Wolf*." 22 March 2008 <http://entertainment.timesonline.co.uk/tol/arts_and_entertainment/stage/theatre/article3576027.ece>.

[8] Source: James Montgomery Flagg, *Roses and Buckshot*, pp. 119, 121, 124.

[9] Source: Barbara Marinacci, *Leading Ladies: A Gallery of Famous Actresses*, pp. 97, 122.

[10] Source: John Miller, *Ralph Richardson*, p. 156.

[11] Source: O. Smith, *Recollections of O. Smith, Comedian*, pp. xv-xvi.

[12] Source: Dick Cavett, "Waiting (and Waiting) in the Wings." *New York Times.* 17 June 2011 <http://nyti.ms/jzFO4r>.

[13] Source: Eli Wallach, *The Good, the Bad, and Me: In My Anecdotage*, p. 118.

[14] Source: Ralph Berry, compiler and editor, *The Methuen Book of Shakespeare Anecdotes*, p. 67.

[15] Source: Robert E. Drennan, ed., *The Algonquin Wits*, p. 144.

[16] Source: Laura Barnett, "Portrait of the Artrist: Paul McGann, actor." *The Guardian*. 3 August 2009 <http://www.guardian.co.uk/culture/2009/aug/03/paul-mcgann-actor>.

[17] Source: Kate Mostel and Madeline Gilford, *170 Years of Show Business*, pp. 164-165.

[18] Source: Peter Hay, *Broadway Anecdotes*, p. 282.

[19] Source: Kenneth Williams, *Acid Drops*, p. 116.

[20] Source: Walter Terry, *Frontiers of Dance: The Life of Martha Graham*, p. 100.

[21] Source: Alistair Cooke, *The Great and the Good*, p. 215.

[22] Source: Anthony Slide, *Eccentrics of Comedy*, p. 131.

[23] Source: Barbara Isenberg, *State of the Arts: California Artists Talk About Their Work*, pp. 115-116.

[24] Source: Art Linkletter, *I Wish I'd Said That!*, p. 37.

[25] Source: Stanley Holloway,*Wiv a Little Bit O' Luck*, pp. 158-159.

[26] Source: Michael Billington, "Michael Billington on theatre refreshments." *The Guardian*. 19 May 2010 <http://www.guardian.co.uk/stage/2010/may/19/critics-notebook-michael-billington>.

[27] Source: Sean McCann, compiler, *The Wit of Brendan Behan*, p. 49.

[28] Source: Lucy Mangan, "Drinking as much as you like is one of the key benefits of being middle-class." *Telegraph* (UK) 24 July 2015 <http://tinyurl.com/pxr2crc>.

[29] Source: Don Nardo, *Greek and Roman Theater*, p. 96.

[30] Source: Richard Huggett, *Supernatural on Stage*, pp. 98-99.

[31] Source: Peter Robinson, "Alice Cooper: 'There are people I'm pretty sure aren't of this planet.'" *Guardian*. 16 September 2015 <http://tinyurl.com/oyn699y>.

[32] Source: Carl Reiner, *My Anecdotal Life*, pp. 133-135.

[33] Source: Ralph Berry, compiler and editor, *The Methuen Book of Shakespeare Anecdotes*, pp. 87-88.

[34] Source: Henry T. Finck, *Musical Laughs*, pp. 56-58.

[35] Source: Margot Fonteyn, *Autobiography*, p. 217.

[36] Source: *Anecdotes of the Hour By Famous Men*, p. 83.

[37] Source: David Ewen, *Listen to the Mocking Words*, pp. 49-50.

[38] Source: John Gielgud and John Miller, *Acting Shakespeare*, p. 44.

[39] Source: Mark Russell, editor, *Out of Character*, p. 33.

[40] Source: Diana Rigg, compiler, *No Turn Unstoned*, p. 168.

[41] Source: Ed McMahon, *Here's Johnny! My Memories of Johnny Carson,* The Tonight Show, *and 46 Years of Friendship*, p. 51.

[42] Source: Roger Ebert, "Ebert's 15th Annual Movie Disaster Awards." *Chicago Sun-Times*. 6 January 1985 <http://rogerebert.suntimes.com/apps/pbcs.dll/article?AID=/19850106/COMMENTARY/902069998>.

[43] Source: Kenneth Williams, *Acid Drops*, p. 141.

[44] Source: Jay Sankey, *Zen and the Art of Stand-Up Comedy*, p. 109.

[45] Source: Everett True, *Hey Ho Let's Go: The Story of the Ramones*, pp. 261, 281, 318-319.

[46] Source: Maurice Zolotow, *No People Like Show People*, p. 15.

[47] Source: Amy Allison, *Shakespeare's Globe*, pp. 41-42.

[48] Source: Barbara Woollcott, *None But a Mule*, pp. 31-33, 36.

[49] Source: Maddy Costa, "A quick curtain call. Then bed: Child actors in adult theatre." *The Guardian*. 5 May 2010 <http://www.guardian.co.uk/stage/2010/may/05/child-actors-interview-jersualem-enron>.

[50] Source: Ruth Turk, *Lillian Hellman: Rebel Playwright*, pp. 18-19, 28.

[51] Source: *Anecdotes of the Hour By Famous Men*, pp. 88-89.

[52] Source: Yousuf Karsh, *Faces of Our Time*, pp. 113-115.

[53] Source: Léonide Massine, *My Life in Ballet*, pp. 15, 100, 149.

[54] Source: Groucho Marx, *Groucho Marx and Other Short Stories and Tall Tales*, pp. 27-29.

[55] Source: Bruce Laffey, *Beatrice Lillie*, pp. 91, 203, 210, 238-239. Also: Michèle Brown and Ann O'Connor, *Hammer and Tongues*, pp. 118-119.

[56] Source: Jay Sankey, *Zen and the Art of Stand-Up Comedy*, p. 45.

[57] Source: "Johnny Cash's Captive Audience." *Neatorama*. 25 July 2014 <http://tinyurl.com/kvyf6fz>.

[58] Source: J. Bryan III, *Merry Gentlemen (and One Lady)*, p. 62.

[59] Source: Anton Dolin, *Alicia Markova: Her Life and Art*, pp. 119-120, 189, 305.

[60]Source: Ted Shawn, *One Thousand and One Night Stands*, pp. 40, 168.

[61]Source: Wendy Neale, *Ballet Life Behind the Scenes*, p. 88.

[62]Source: Wendy Neale, *Ballet Life Behind the Scenes*, pp. 90.

[63]Source: Ted Shawn, *One Thousand and One Night Stands*, p. 265.

[64] Source: Walter Rowland, *Among the Great Masters of the Drama*, p. 82.

[65] Source: Joan Oliver Goldsmith, *How Can We Keep from Singing: Music and the Passionate Life*, pp. 143, 151-152.

[66]Source: Robin May, compiler, *The Wit of the Theatre*, pp. 94, 100, 103-104.

[67] Source: Frank Lovece, "Fyvush Finkel: the face that launched a thousand shticks." *Newsday*. 9 January 2008 <http://www.popmatters.com/pm/news/article/52916/fyvush-finkel-the-face-that-launched-a-thousand-shticks/>.

[68]Source: Alexander Woollcott, *Enchanted Aisles*, pp. 229-231, 233.

[69]Source: Ben Hecht, *Charlie: The Improbable Life and Times of Charles MacArthur*, p. 163.

[70]Source: Robert E. Drennan, ed., *The Algonquin Wits*, pp. 15, 62. Also: Alexander Woollcott, *Shouts and Murmurs*, p. 85.

[71] Source: Dick Cavett, "The Titan and the Pfc." *The New York Times*. 8 October 2010 <http://opinionator.blogs.nytimes.com/2010/10/08/the-titan-and-the-pfc/?ref=opinion>.

[72]Source: Hesketh Pearson, *Lives of the Wits*, pp. 197, 209.

[73]Source: John Gielgud, *Distinguished Company*, p. 63.

[74] Source: Danny Newman, *Tales of a Theatrical Guru*, p. 77.

[75] Source: Henry T. Finck, *My Adventures in the Golden Age of Music*, p. 253.

[76]Source: Sam Norkin, *Drawings, Stories*, p. 250.

[77]Source: Diana Rigg, compiler, *No Turn Unstoned*, p. 99.

[78]Source: H. Allen Smith, *The Compleat Practical Joker*, pp. 166-167.

[79] Source: Henry T. Finck, *My Adventures in the Golden Age of Music*, p. 345.

[80]Source: Peter Hay, *Broadway Anecdotes*, p. 179.

[81]Source: John Gielgud and John Miller, *Acting Shakespeare*, p. 124.

[82]Source: Alexander Woollcott, *Shouts and Murmurs*, p. 86.

[83]Source: Dick Richards, compiler, *The Wit of Noël Coward*, p. 44.

[84] Source: John Rankin Towse, *Sixty Years of the Theater: An Old Critic's Memories*, p. 17.

[85] Source: Alicia Markova, *Markova Remembers*, pp. 10, 24, 58, 100-101.

[86] Source: Carin T. Ford, *Legends of American Dance and Choreography*, pp. 15, 27, 67, 96.

[87] Source: Margaret F. Atkinson and May Hillman, *Dancers of the Ballet*, pp. 7, 116, 142, 151.

[88] Source: Walter Terry, *Ted Shawn: Father of American Dance*, pp. 63, 92-93, 135-136, 174.

[89] Source: Rose Eichenbaum, *Masters of Movement: Portraits of America's Great Choreographers*, p. 111.

[90] Source: Robert Greskovic, *Ballet 101*, pp. 67, 124, 171, 361.

[91] Source: Holly Brubach, *Ten Dancers*, pp. 35, 57, 81.

[92] Source: Jim Haskins and N.R. Mitgang, *Mr. Bojangles*, pp. 18, 101, 167.

[93] Source: Sarah Montague, *Pas de Deux*, pp. 14, 69, 83, 89.

[94] Source: Natalia Makarova, *A Dance Autobiography*, pp. 77, 120.

[95] Source: Sarah Montague, *Pas de Deux*, pp. 23, 41, 48, 57.

[96] Source: Suzanne Farrell, *Holding On to the Air*, p. 233.

[97] Source: Nicolas Legat, *Ballet Russe*, p. 27.

[98] Source: Susan Suntree, *Rita Moreno*, p. 34.

[99] Source: John Miller, *Judi Dench: With a Crack in Her Voice*, p. 215.

[100] Source: Gerald Nachman, *Seriously Funny*, pp. 138, 147.

[101] Source: Nancy Durrant, "The V&A: talking 'bout my inspiration." *The Times*. 10 March 2009 <http://entertainment.timesonline.co.uk/tol/arts_and_entertainment/stage/article5876668.ece>.

[102] Source: Stephen M. Silverman, *Funny Ladies*, p. 33.

[103] Source: Eddie Cantor and David Freedman, *Ziegfeld: The Great Glorifier*, p. 77.

[104] Source: Nick Harris, *I Wish I'd Said That!*, p. 100.

[105] Source: "Peter Ustinov." June 2007 <http://en.wikipedia.org/wiki/Peter_Ustinov>.

[106] Source: Jon Ronson, "The Frank Sidebottom Oh Blimey Big Band." *Guardian*. 30 May 2006 <http://tinyurl.com/nwcube4>.

[107] Source: Barbara Woollcott, *None But a Mule*, pp. 142-143, 151.

[108] Source: Anton Dolin, *Alicia Markova: Her Life and Art*, pp. 126-127, 159-160.

[109] Source: Valerie Grove, "Legend of the lady in a brown party dress." *The Times*. 14 December 2002 <http://www.timesonline.co.uk/tol/life_and_style/article801488.ece>.

[110] Source: Eli Wallach, *The Good, the Bad, and Me: In My Anecdotage*, p. 117.

[111] Source: Anna Russell, *I'm Not Making This Up, You Know*, pp. 2, 60.

[112] Source: Rose Eichenbaum, *Masters of Movement: Portraits of America's Great Choreographers*, pp. 125, 127.

[113] Source: Dick Richards, compiler, *The Wit of Peter Ustinov*, p. 18.

[114] Source: John Miller, *Ralph Richardson*, p. 164.

[115] Source: Michèle Brown and Ann O'Connor, *Hammer and Tongues*, p. 116.

[116] Source: Milt Hinton, David G. Berger, and Holly Maxson, *Playing the Changes: Milt Hinton's Life in Stories and Photographs*, p. 279.

[117] Source: Constance Benson, *Mainly Players*, p. 242.

[118] Source: Carl Reiner, *My Anecdotal Life*, pp. 179-181.

[119] Source: Alexandra Danilova, *Choura*, pp. 8, 73.

[120] Source: Stanley Holloway, *Wiv a Little Bit O' Luck*, p. 192.

[121] Source: Eddie Cantor and David Freedman, *Ziegfeld: The Great Glorifier*, pp. 42-43.

[122] Source: Art Linkletter, *I Wish I'd Said That!*, p. 64.

[123] Source: Joan Oliver Goldsmith, *How Can We Keep from Singing: Music and the Passionate Life*, pp. 99, 116.

[124] Source: Dominic Wells, "Rocky Horror? It was about my mother." *The Times*. 18 August 2009 <http://entertainment.timesonline.co.uk/tol/arts_and_entertainment/stage/theatre/article6799279.ece>. Also: Caroline Scot, "Best of times, worst of times: Richard O'Brien, creator of 'The Rocky Horror Show.'" *The Times*. 22 June 2003)

[125] Source: Duane Well, "Levi Kreis Finds Where He Belongs." *The Advocate*. 17 September 2009 <http://www.advocate.com/Arts_and_Entertainment/Music/Levi_Kreis_Finds_Where_He_Belongs/>.

[126] Source: James Montgomery Flagg, *Roses and Buckshot*, pp. 36-37.

[127] Source: Herbert Block, *Herblock: A Cartoonist's Life*, p. 383.

[128] Source: John Drew, *My Years on the Stage*, pp. 81, 83.

[129] Source: John Drew, *My Years on the Stage*, pp. 63-64.

[130] Source: Stephen Tanner, *Opera Antics and Anecdotes*, pp. 83-84.

[131] Source: Suzanne Farrell, *Holding On to the Air*, p. 172.

[132] Source: Andrew Gumbel, "If there's one thing I'm prepared for, it's rejection." *The Guardian*. 21 October 2009 <http://www.guardian.co.uk/lifeandstyle/2009/oct/21/jeremy-piven-entourage-the-goods>.

[133] Source: Joe Queenan, "Born to Be Blue: Ethan Hawke on the fast life and mysterious death of Chet Baker." *Guardian*. 20 July 2016 <http://tinyurl.com/gvazc5n>.

[134] Source: Alan Wagner, *Prima Donnas and Other Wild Beasts*, p. 1.

[135] Source: Sean McCann, compiler, *The Wit of Brendan Behan*, p. 46.

[136] Source: Dick Richards, compiler, *The Wit of Noël Coward*, pp. 56-57.

[137] Source: Julie Burchill, "Bring back the red-blooded bitch." *The Guardian*. 4 January 2008 <http://www.guardian.co.uk/g2/story/0,,2235197,00.html>.

[138] Source: Nick Harris, *I Wish I'd Said That!*, p. 153.

[139] Source: Susan Cavett, *Talk Show: Confrontations, Pointed Commentary, and Off-Screen Secrets*, pp. 238-239.

[140] Source: Ruth Turk, *Lillian Hellman: Rebel Playwright*, pp. 87, 120-121.

[141] Source: Lewis C. Henry, *Humorous Anecdotes About Famous People*, p. 112.

[142] Source: Ben Hecht, *Charlie: The Improbable Life and Times of Charles MacArthur*, p. 92.

[143] Source: Lewis C. Henry, *Humorous Anecdotes About Famous People*, p. 1.

[144] Source: David W. Barber, *When the Fat Lady Sings*, p. 36.

[145] Source: William Donaldson, *Great Disasters of the Stage*, p. 104.

[146]Source: Barrymore Laurence Scherer, *Bravo! A Guide to Opera for the Perplexed*, p. 85.

[147]Source: Maurice Zolotow, *No People Like Show People*, p. 263.

[148]Source: H. Allen Smith, *To Hell in a Handbasket*, pp. 202-203.

[149]Source: Alexander Woollcott, *Enchanted Aisles*, p. 152.

[150]Source: Holly Hughes, *Clit Notes: A Sapphic Sampler*, p. 184.

[151] Source: *Reflections: The Taper at Twenty*, pp. 55, 95, 103.

[152]Source: Plácido Domingo, *My First Forty Years*, pp. 57, 101, 135.

[153] Source: Paul Arendt, Anita Sethi and Dave Simpson, interviewers. "'If that goes off again I'll kill you.'" *The Guardian*. 11 September 2008 <http://www.guardian.co.uk/stage/2008/sep/11/comedy>.

[154]Source: Alicia Markova, *Giselle and Me*, pp. 53-54, 75-76, 148.

[155] Source: Susan Suntree, *Rita Moreno*, pp. 70-71.

[156]Source: Barry Hewlett-Davies, *A Night at the Opera*, pp. 29, 41, 106.

[157]Source: Jerome K. Jerome, *On the Stage—and Off*, p. 66.

[158]Source: Margot Fonteyn, *Autobiography*, pp.189-190, 216.

[159]Source: Robert Morley, *Robert Morley's Book of Bricks*, pp. 137-138.

[160]Source: Jack and Waltraud Karkar, compilers and editors, ... *And They Danced On*, pp. 195-196.

[161]Source: Robert Morley, *Robert Morley's Book of Bricks*, pp. 63, 116.

[162]Source: Gyles Brandreth, *Great Theatrical Disasters*, p. 25.

[163]Source: Alexandra Danilova, *Choura*, p. 120.

[164]Source: Illaria Obidenna Ladré, *Illaria Obidenna Ladré: Memoirs of a Child of Theatre Street*, p. 24.

[165]Source: Victor Borge and Robert Sherman, *My Favorite Intermissions*, p. 32.

[166]Source: Agnes de Mille, *Portrait Gallery*, p. 97.

[167]Source: H. Allen Smith, *To Hell in a Handbasket*, p. 298.

[168] Source: Kenn Duncan, *Divas: The Fabulous Photography of Kenn Duncan*, p. 215.

[169]Source: Mark Russell, editor, *Out of Character*, p. 217.

[170]Source: Alicia Markova, *Markova Remembers*, pp. 150-151.

[171]Source: Frank Ernest Nicholson, *Favorite Jokes of Famous People*, pp. 42-43.

[172]Source: David W. Barber, *When the Fat Lady Sings*, p. 46.

[173] Source: Milt Hinton, David G. Berger, and Holly Maxson, *Playing the Changes: Milt Hinton's Life in Stories and Photographs*, pp. 238-239.

[174]Source: Leon A. Harris, *The Fine Art of Political Wit*, p. 40.

[175] Source: Susan King, "Boris Karloff, a monster talent remembered[1]." Latimes.com. 30 August 2010 < http://latimesblogs.latimes.com/herocomplex/ 2010/08/boris-karloff-a-monster-talent-remembered.html>.

[176] Source: Frances Alda, *Men, Women, and Tenors*, p. 116.

[177]Source: Helen L. Kaufmann, *Anecdotes of Music and Musicians*, pp. 68-69.

[178]Source: Barbara Marinacci, *Leading Ladies: A Gallery of Famous Actresses*, p. 34.

[179] Source: Danny Newman, *Tales of a Theatrical Guru*, p. 70.

[180]Source: Alexandra Danilova, *Choura*, p. 85.

[181]Source: Colonel J. H. Mapleson, *The Mapleson Memoirs*, p. 103.

[182]Source: Frank Ernest Nicholson, *Favorite Jokes of Famous People*, pp. 150-151.

[183]Source: Plácido Domingo, *My First Forty Years*, p. 172.

[184]Source: David W. Barber, *If It Ain't Baroque...*, pp. 44, 81, 95, 104.

[185]Source: Laning Humphrey, compiler, *The Humor of Music and Other Oddities in the Art*, pp. 35, 52, 56.

[186]Source: Thomas Beecham, *A Mingled Chime*, p. 291.

[187]Source: Alicia Markova, *Giselle and Me*, pp. 58, 123.

[188]Source: Robert Greskovic, *Ballet 101*, pp. 25, 29.

[189]Source: Alistair Cooke, *The Great and the Good*, p. 210.

[190] Source: Sheela Lambert, "The Man Behind the Hair." *The Advocate*. 13 August 2008 <http://www.advocate.com/exclusive_detail_ektid59252.asp>.

[191]Source: Gyles Brandreth, *Great Theatrical Disasters*, p. 134.

[192] Source: Kenn Duncan, *Divas: The Fabulous Photography of Kenn Duncan*, p. 205.

---

1.   http://latimesblogs.latimes.com/herocomplex/2010/08/boris-karloff-a-monster-talent-remembered.html

[193] Source: Maria Raha, *Cinderella's Big Score*, pp. 33-34, 48, 62, 68, 88, 140-41, 145.

[194] Source: Andrew Tobias, "Strike the Band Up." 22 June 2009 <http://www.andrewtobias.com/newcolumns/090622.html>.

[195] Source: Agnes de Mille, *Portrait Gallery*, p. 216.

[196] Source: Sean McCann, compiler, *The Wit of the Irish*, pp. 93-95.

[197] Source: Theodore Stier, *With Pavlova Around the World*, p. 271.

[198] Source: Sean McCann, compiler, *The Wit of Brendan Behan*, pp. 49, 80-81, 121.

[199] Source: Leon A. Harris, *The Fine Art of Political Wit*, p, 23.

[200] Source: Maxwell Yezpitelok, "4 Legendary Pranks Pulled Off by Celebrities." *Cracked*. 30 March 2014 <http://tinyurl.com/pkslbmt>.

[201] Source: H. Allen Smith, *The Compleat Practical Joker*, p. 178.

[202] Source: Dick Richards, compiler, *The Wit of Peter Ustinov*, pp. 97-98.

[203] Source: Walter Rowland, *Among the Great Masters of the Drama*, pp. 90-91.

[204] Source: Jim Haskins and N.R. Mitgang, *Mr. Bojangles*, p. 228.

[205] Source: Catherine Scheader, *Lorraine Hansberry: Playwright and Voice of Justice*, p. 77.

[206] Source: John W. Crawford, *Early Shakespearean Actresses*, pp. 82-83.

[207] Source: Henry T. Finck, *Musical Laughs*, pp. 54-55.

[208] Source: John Rankin Towse, *Sixty Years of the Theater: An Old Critic's Memories*, pp. 366-367.

[209] Source: Herbert Block, *Herblock: A Cartoonist's Life*, p. 138.

[210] Source: Stephen Tanner, *Opera Antics and Anecdotes*, pp. 84-85.

[211] Source: Amy Allison, *Shakespeare's Globe*, pp. 24-27.

[212] Source: Alan Wagner, *Prima Donnas and Other Wild Beasts*, pp. 73-74.

[213] Source: Victor Borge and Robert Sherman, *My Favorite Intermissions*, p. 104.

[214] Source: John Miller, *Judi Dench: With a Crack in Her Voice*, p. 220.

[215] Source: Anna Russell, *I'm Not Making This Up, You Know*, p. 174.

[216] Source: Constance Benson, *Mainly Players*, pp. 107-108.

[217] Source: Helen L. Kaufmann, *Anecdotes of Music and Musicians*, pp. 109-112.

[218]Source: John W. Crawford, *Early Shakespearean Actresses*, pp. 89-90.

[219] Source: Leo Benedictus, "Is it ever a good idea to 'have a go'?" *The Guardian*. 2 October 2008 <http://www.guardian.co.uk/uk/2008/oct/02/ukcrime1>.

[220]Source: Frances Alda, *Men, Women, and Tenors*, p. 93.

[221] Source: William Donaldson, *Great Disasters of the Stage*, p. 4.

[222]Source: Julien Phillips, *Stars of the Ziegfeld Follies*, p. 23.

[223]Source: Julien Phillips, *Stars of the Ziegfeld Follies*, pp. 29-30.

[224]Source: David Ewen, *Listen to the Mocking Words*, p. 18.

[225]Source: Robin May, compiler, *The Wit of the Theatre*, p. 54.

[226]Source: Leo Slezak, *Song of Motley*, pp. 41-42.

[227]Source: Sean McCann, compiler, *The Wit of the Irish*, p. 124.

[228] Source: John Gielgud, *Distinguished Company*, pp. 92-93.

[229] Source: Groucho Marx, *Groucho Marx and Other Short Stories and Tall Tales*, pp. 30-33.

[230]Source: Spike Milligan, *Adolf Hitler: My Part in His Downfall*, pp. 64-65.

[231]Source: Richard Huggett, *Supernatural on Stage*, pp. 19, 43, 57.

[232]Source: Samuel Marx, *Broadway Portraits*, pp. 11, 16, 20.

[233]Source: Stephen M. Silverman, *Funny Ladies*, p. 92.

[234]Source: Colonel J. H. Mapleson, *The Mapleson Memoirs*, p. 64.

[235] Source: Yousuf Karsh, *Faces of Our Time*, pp. 101-103.

[236]Source: Sir Rudolf Bing, *5000 Nights at the Opera*, p. 260.

[237]Source: Illaria Obidenna Ladré, *Illaria Obidenna Ladré: Memoirs of a Child of Theatre Street*, pp. 29, 36-38.

[238]Source: Graham Chapman, *Graham Crackers*, p. 151.

[239]Source: J. Bryan III, *Merry Gentlemen (and One Lady)*, pp. 128. 136-137.

[240]Source: Holly Hughes, *Clit Notes: A Sapphic Sampler*, pp. 75, 157, 163-164.

[241] Source: Martyn Palmer, "I've been alone most of my life...." *The Times*. 21 July 2007 <http://entertainment.timesonline.co.uk/tol/arts_and_entertainment/film/article2065586.ece>.

[242]Source: Hesketh Pearson, *Lives of the Wits*, pp. 91, 120.

[243] Source: Andre Maurois, "An Appreciation," introduction to Voltaire, *Candide*, pp. 2-3.

[244] Source: O. Smith, *Recollections of O. Smith, Comedian*, p. 53.

[245] Source: Sam Norkin, *Drawings, Stories*, p. 51.

[246] Source: Sir Rudolf Bing, *5000 Nights at the Opera*, pp. 8-9, 131.

[247] Source: Jeremy Nichols, "Introduction" of Jerome K. Jerome's *On the Stage—and Off*, p. xiii.

[248] Source: Jack and Waltraud Karkar, compilers and editors, ... *And They Danced On*, p. 172.

[249] Source: Rusty E. Frank, *Tap!*, p. 255.

[250] Source: Thomas Beecham, *A Mingled Chime*, pp. 134-135.

[251] Source: Spike Milligan, *Adolf Hitler: My Part in His Downfall*, p. 32.

[252] Source: Leo Slezak, *Song of Motley*, p. 50.

[253] Source: Rusty E. Frank, *Tap!*, pp. 144-145.

[254] Source: Kate Mostel and Madeline Gilford, *170 Years of Show Business*, p. 11.

[255] Source: Catherine Scheader, *Lorraine Hansberry: Playwright and Voice of Justice*, p. 46.

[256] Source: Barrymore Laurence Scherer, *Bravo! A Guide to Opera for the Perplexed*, p. 248.

www.ingramcontent.com/pod-product-compliance
Lightning Source LLC
Chambersburg PA
CBHW032020140726
47988CB00017BA/841